China Bound

Thelma Notley

Woman's Missionary Union
Birmingham, Alabama

Woman's Missionary Union
P. O. Box 830010
Birmingham, AL 35283-0010

Dewey Decimal Classification: 266.51
Subject Headings: MISSIONS—CHINA
                  NOTLEY, LOREN
                  NOTLEY, THELMA

Design by Janell E. Young

ISBN: 1-56309-741-9
W994143•0999•5M1

To Karen Mitchell

God Bless You!

Thelma Notley

For Loren
For whom China was the crowning work of his life

Contents

1: The China Bound Trunk 3

2: Faraway Places 10

3: Riding the Iron Rooster 18

4: Dongbei on the Hill 25

5: Hai Shi Jiao 31

6: Popcorn and Chicken Soup 41

7: Between the Garden and the Gate 52

8: Sir, We Would See Jesus 58

9: The Three-Self Church 65

10: Opening Doors .71

11: Only Love and English Spoken Here 76

12: The Buddhist Bell 84

13: Coke and Christian Conversation 88

14: China Thanksgiving 93

15: Making Disciples 102

16: Christmas 108

17: China Call 112

18: China Joy 126

19: Tiananmen Square 136

20: Har Shalom 147

21: Aslan Is on the Move 154

22: I Touch the Scales 166

23: For China and for Thee 172

China Bound

Today I put my foot on China's sand.
I turned my back on verdant hills of home.
I touched "the Wall" that for eons did stand
Between her people and "eternal song."

"Come spend the coin of love I give," He says,
"And with My grace, buy China for My own.
Inherit all the uttermost parts of earth.
Your life of joy in me has just begun."

I see the "mei li" faces of the youth,
The bright, expectant laughter of the child,
The hungry gaze within an elder's eyes;
I knew, *I knew* the answer all the while!

Oh, Lord, I leave it gladly all behind,
The home I love, my children running free.
Eternal things hang balanced in Your hand.
I touch the scales for China, and for Thee.

—Thelma Notley

1

The China Bound Trunk

The wrinkled old trunk, recently arrived from India, had held beloved keepsakes of a family returning after years on the missions field. Now it sat empty, pushed out of the way, its task completed, its days of usefulness over. Or were they?

"We need crates—lots of crates—to get all this stuff to China," my husband said with concern.

Retired schoolteachers in our 60s, Loren and I were preparing to go to China to teach English. We knew enough about the austerity of life in China, with its lack of creature comforts, to know that we needed to send household provisions and teaching materials ahead.

Learning of our dilemma, our missionary friends graciously offered us the old trunk. Even then, not all our problems were solved. What should we pack in the trunk, and what should we leave behind?

"Why do you want to take all this stuff anyway?" Loren asked.

"They are things we'll need!"

"I thought the idea was to live as the Chinese do. You know, 'when in Rome . . .'"

"We'll need a few things from home to help us recover from culture shock," I reasoned.

Culture shock! What a horrible phrase! It was enough to give a person second thoughts about going to another country.

"OK," he relented. "I agree about the dry foods, popcorn, and the Autoharp for our private worship time. But an electric blanket? Come on, now. Get real!"

Now I was *really* on the defensive and ready to do battle.

"You know I won't sleep if I'm cold. I'll be miserable and I'll never overcome culture shock. If you're taking cowboy boots and all those boxes of oatmeal, I'm taking the blanket!"

Fair was fair, and the matter was settled.[1]

♦

My parents had been missionaries to Nigeria where two of my siblings and I were born, and I have come to believe that missions is in the blood. After returning home from Nigeria it had been their prayer that God would call one of their children to follow in their footsteps and "go back to Africa." All through my childhood my family talked of it, often feeling that God was calling first one and then another of their children to go back. But not me.

When other young people were kneeling at the altar at summer camp or during revivals, answering God's call on their lives to go into ministry or to the missions field, I felt left out.

"Why isn't God calling me?" I wondered to my mother.

With gentle understanding she asked me, "What do you think God is calling you to do?"

Although missions had always had a heavy pull on my heart, my dream was of China, not Africa.

It was the 1940s, war raged in China, and the country was closed. So my dream of China had slipped into some shadowy recess of my heart.

"I just want to get married and have a family," was my teenaged answer. Then Mother spoke the words of wisdom that guided me for the rest of my life.

"If you can marry a godly man and raise a godly family, that is the greatest call God can put on the life of a woman."

And she released me to be and do what God had for me to do.

So, for many years I dreamed secretly of China, and my life took on the normalcy of being wife, mother, and teacher.

Obtaining an education, raising a family of four, being the "efficient" wife of a school administrator, carrying a full-time teaching load, and accepting places of responsibility in my church left little time for dreaming. I had chosen my life. It wasn't particularly easy, but it was the call of God, I believed, and I was determined to be faithful in all He had called me to do.

But, somewhere in a hidden corner of my soul lingered the dream of China and the forgotten yearning to go to the missions field.

We had taken a family vacation to the Southwest and had planned a stopover at our church's retreat center at Glorieta, New Mexico. It just happened to be Foreign Missions Week. We sat in the large tabernacle, listening as the president of the Foreign Mission Board (now International Mission Board) preached a powerful message calling whole families to surrender to go to "fields white unto harvest." When an invitation was given, I watched in awe as young couples, taking their children by the hands, moved down the aisles and knelt in surrender to the call God had placed on their lives.

6

It was too much for my hungry heart. I began to weep. I could not control the sobs that wracked my body. It was as if the whole world was following after God, and I was being left behind. But God saw those tears of yearning. He knew of my longing to go to China. God had put it there in my childhood, and only He could remove it.

Busy years followed. Working to rear, teach, and help support the children and eventually helping them to go to college was my life. Family altars at the breakfast table every morning and a very active participation in all church activities rounded out our lives. We had been commanded to bring up our children in "the fear and admonition of the Lord." He had promised that if we were faithful in this, that "when they are old, they will not depart from it," a promise He has kept.

God was faithful in His part of this bargain between us. All four of our children married and established Christian homes. Our two sons were called to the missions field. Dan and his family were called to Thailand. Steve and his family went to Israel.

Once when Steve was still in college, struggling with God's call on his life, gripped with the strong pull of missions and weeping over the lost in India, I reminded him of the prayers of his grandparents.

"Perhaps you are the answer to their prayers," I said. Hearing the story again as if for the first time, he leapt and shouted, "Glory! I've got 50 years of prayer behind me!"

But my own love of missions and the sweet dream of China remained hidden somewhere in my heart.

Then in 1972 Richard Nixon went to China, stood on the Great Wall, and opened the door of China to the West. God was getting ready to give me the desires of my heart.

♦

"Thelma, look at this thing on my neck!"

It was early morning and Loren and I were in the steamy bathroom getting ready to go to school. As Loren shaved, he noticed a small lump on his neck just above the hollow of his collar bone. It was as soft and malleable as a cotton ball.

"What do you think it is?" I asked.

"I don't know, but I'm going to see the doctor. I want it off!" he declared.

"It's only a fatty tumor," reassured the doctor. "It 's not dangerous at all."

"I don't care," Loren said stubbornly. "Anything that comes up that fast on me, I want off."

So a minor lumpectomy was scheduled for early New Year's Day. He would be home in time for the football games, the doctor assured him. But the doctor was wrong. Not about the fatty tumor. In that, he was correct. It *was* just a fatty tumor. But near the harmless tumor were two darkened lymph nodes that turned out to be malignant. *Loren had lymphoma!*

We had finished our responsibilities to our children who were all married and busy with lives of their own. For several years we had been spending our vacation time building a home on the lake. We were happily looking forward to retirement there. Now, the future didn't look so exciting.

But into this picture came some news that *was* exciting! China had opened its doors to teachers of English as a second language. It was inviting hundreds of American teachers to come at China's expense to teach in its colleges and universities.

We were teachers.

We were ready to retire.

We were free to go.

CHINA!

Here was my dream at last! But Loren had cancer.

However, "demon cancer" didn't understand who he was dealing with. Twenty years before, the Lord had healed me of leiomyosarcoma, a virulent form of cancer. We believed in God's ability to heal. And Loren was never one to quit if he wanted something badly enough.

So he went for his first treatments; soon doctors could find no trace of lymphoma. They decided that it had been a misdiagnosis. It wasn't cancer at all. They believed they had made a mistake. But we believed God had healed him.

With great rejoicing we prepared to go to China.

We took a short course in Mandarin and joined a Christian organization that placed teachers in China.

"The Chinese are going to *love* you two," exclaimed the wife of the organization's director, looking at our white hair.

Through them we received our assignment. We got our passports and shipped our trunk.

But Satan had another arrow to throw our way.

The week before departure, through means of a report on my mammogram, I was informed that I had a lump in my breast.

"That devil!" I exclaimed when the doctor informed me of the report. In response to his shocked look, for he thought I was addressing him, I explained.

"The devil will do anything to keep us from going to China."

Angry and discouraged, we consulted a surgeon who examined the X ray. He pointed to a tiny spot high up on my shoulder.

"It's probably genetic," he said. "You may have had it from birth."

"What shall we do?" I asked.

"You have two choices," he said. "I can remove the cyst, or you can go to China and come back to see me next year."

"We'll go to China," we exclaimed joyfully.

So we packed our bags, kissed our family good-bye, and boarded the plane for China.

We had beaten Old Slew Foot!

------

[1]Thelma A. Notley, "Sir, We Would See Jesus," *Confident Living,* February 1993.

2

Faraway Places

L oren had been something of a world traveler, having served in both the navy and the army, his traveling courtesy of Uncle Sam. But I had not. I think I must have always had "itchy feet." I yearned to travel. A little song about faraway places danced in my head continuously. But since returning from Africa, I had never really been anywhere much outside of Oklahoma. At the time of my first airplane flight I was 53 years old. Never ones to do things moderately, for my first flight we flew halfway around the world to visit Dan and his family in Thailand (Siam). The little song was coming true.

Shortly after takeoff, Loren excused himself and left his seat. When he returned a message came over the intercom, "Congratulations to 'first flighter' Thelma Notley." Always the clown, Loren was in cahoots with the stewardess. Soon they came bringing me not the wings they usually give children, but a deck of playing cards and a magnum of champagne—great gifts but not appropriate for one raised as a noncardplaying, teetotaling Southern Baptist.

Upon arrival at Dan's home in Thailand, I was in a quandary about what to do with my champagne. As a missionary, Dan could not give it to his neighbor because he spoke against strong drink and his own witness would not allow it. Not knowing what to do with it, I wrapped it in a sweater and put it in the bottom of my suitcase.

Our American daughter-in-law is an extremely thorough housekeeper. So are most of the Thai people, who discard their shoes at the door and enter their homes in their stocking feet. The family had a maid who not only swept the house, but actually washed all the floors every day. There was never anything unclean on the floors.

In spite of this, we seemed to have a lot of ants up on second floor and they all appeared to be making trails to my suitcase. Following the trail, I found that the champagne had popped its cork in the Thai heat. We had the happiest colony of ants in Thailand.

Loren poured the wine down the toilet.

We kept the cards.

◆

Now we were on our way to China.

We left Tulsa International Airport with our sponsoring organization, stopping over briefly in Denver where I was able to say good-bye to my sister and her husband. Our luggage had been checked through en masse under the name of our director.

We arrived in Beijing shortly after midnight. Being ushered royally through the crowds of staring Chinese, our arrival seemed almost painless and not the hassle we had expected. Checking through customs was a breeze. We simply walked through, the first and last time that ever happened to us in China. Our hassle was yet to come.

As each family group or couple exited customs, their names were called out, and they stepped into the welcoming arms of waiting Foreign Affairs representatives from their various universities who now became their hosts. They were then swept off to accommodations in the finest Beijing hotels. But not so the Notleys.

After all the others had disappeared, we were left standing alone. Our representative had never arrived. Angry and embarrassed, the head of the national Bureau of Foreign Affairs of the People's Republic of China loaded our luggage into his van and took us with him.

The midnight ride from the airport to our hotel through the dark streets of Beijing became indelibly imprinted on my mind. I sat with my nose pressed against the van window peering into the night. Although there were very few streetlights, our driver did not turn on the van lights. Someone later explained this strange practice to us. The Chinese believe that by driving without headlights they are conserving energy, always in short supply in China.

Riding through the dark and silent night, I was able to drink in the lovely sight of the tall poplar trees that lined the roadway. We felt alone and transported to some magical world we had dreamed about for so long. A more romantic and mysterious welcome to China I cannot imagine.

The secretary of the bureau took us to the International Friendship Hotel, where he personally checked us into our room. The representative from our university did not appear until the next day. But we could not really be angry. We had received the attention of the highest level of authority in the Chinese government. It seemed a portent of things to come.

Jet lag had, of course, set in. Yet I could not sleep for the strangeness and excitement of actually being in China. Far into the night I sat at the window and watched the street below me in the gentle twilight of the August sky. Soft bells rang in the distance, conjuring up mysterious and romantic images, until I finally discerned that they were bicycle bells of people going to work in the early, predawn hours.

Never mind! I was in China at last!

The next morning we solved the mystery of the missing university Foreign Affairs representative. The man from our school had preferred not to come, a decision I am sure he later regretted, as he was soon replaced. It was quite obvious to all that even though he was in charge of Foreign Affairs at our school, he resented the foreign teachers. Instead of coming to meet us himself, he took a holiday and sent a young woman from his department. Unfortunately, Ann had gotten sidetracked the night before. She had spent the night with a "friend." And from the looks of her very rumpled dress, it was easy for us to discern why she had been otherwise occupied.

Breakfast that morning was our initiation into Chinese cuisine. Whatever I thought of the food then, I now know that it was a very exceptional breakfast for China.

We met in the dining room with others of our group who were staying in the Friendship Hotel. We were offered tea, of course, but no coffee. Eggs, toast, butter, and jelly were the main course, but there was also cabbage soup and rice. Pickles and peanuts at breakfast were something of a shock to us. Loren would have preferred oatmeal and I would have relished buckwheat pancakes. But we ate with good spirits and were satisfied.

Poor Ann had not had such an easy morning. Before we saw her, the national director had "called her on the carpet" to give an account of her absence. Nevertheless, it had done little good. She resented us from the start even though we were her reason for being in Beijing. She had no interest in caring for us as she was supposed to do. When other representatives were taking their new teachers sight-seeing in that great city, Ann told us to hire a guide and a taxi, and left us to ourselves.

At first we were frustrated, and a little frightened, at being left alone in a strange place where we could not speak the language and did not understand the culture of the people. "I have wanted to come to China all my life!" I fumed. "Are we just going to sit here and let Satan spoil this time for us? We may never have a chance to see Beijing again!"

Satan had tried to keep us out of China. We knew God took us there for a purpose. We would not let Satan rob us of this wonderful opportunity. We would not spend the day moping in the hotel room feeling sorry for ourselves.

Doing exactly as Ann had suggested, we took a taxi to the Forbidden City where we had our first experience with what we later came to refer to as our "Chinese angels."

Many of China's younger people are obsessed with learning English in the hope of going to America on business. They often go out of their way to assist Americans in order to practice their English. And so it was with us that first day in China.

A handsome young man saw us emerge from our taxi at the steps to the Forbidden City and came to our rescue. The rest of the day we were in his care, a very gracious "angel" he turned out to be. What had seemed to be the start of a hopeless and wasted day was made much richer because he had offered to be our guide.

The Imperial Palace, known as the Forbidden City, is immense. During the days of the ruling monarchs, no one except the royal family and the servants could enter, under penalty of death. After the disposition of Pu Yi, the last of the Qing emperors, the Imperial Palace became a museum. Today, most of the city is open to the public. What little of the city we saw was very old and had the look of desertion and the feel of decay.

In the evening we took another taxi and went to see the lovely and exotic Summer Palace of the empress dowager Cixi. Situated on the shore of beautiful Lake Dian Chi, its stone and marble buildings have been rebuilt several times because of damage they sustained during the toppling of regimes and power struggles within the government. Today, beautifully restored, they are magnificent.

It was a sultry day, but cool breezes blew off the waters of the lake and made the park and the walks through the gardens very refreshing. Great masses of water lilies lay along the shore. In the distance, "floating" on the waters of the lake, was an "ivory boat." The boat, of stone, provided the empress with a cool retreat on very warm days, reachable by a causeway. As it was late in the day, we did not have time to "go sailing" on the empress's boat.

"Another time," we said. But seldom, if ever, do the other times come. And they did not come for us. God had more important things for us to see and do in China.

Poor Ann! Because of her neglect of us that second day, she was in even more hot water. She received an ultimatum. Though she resented us, she must remain with us for the rest of our time in Beijing, friend or no friend. Stubbornly she would only do so when we were with the entire group. The other Foreign Affairs representatives took us under their wings, letting her know that she had shamed them all. Even in our presence, they were not very kind to her. Ann's initial rejection of us, and the rejection of her by her director and fellow agents, created huge stumbling blocks to her openness to God's love. Loren and I were never able to reach Ann.

On our last day in Beijing, we traveled by bus to see the famous Ming Tombs and the Great Wall of China. The Ling'en Hall in Changling Tomb was built in 1427 as a place where emperors, empresses, and civil and military officials could pay homage or offer sacrifices to their ancestors.

Built between 1584 and 1590, the Dingling Tomb served as a "longevity palace" for the then reigning Emperor Wan Li when he was 23. Thirty-five years later he was dead. So much for his longevity. As with the Taj Mahal, these beautiful and extravagant palaces are wasted on the dead. We have no need for such places. We worship a Living Lord.

Finally, we got to visit the Great Wall of China. What a magnificent work of man it is! One of the seven wonders of the ancient world, it is said to be the only man-made structure on earth that can be seen from outer space.

What a day we had! We climbed the steep steps and the inclining walks which seemed to undulate over the rolling hillsides. One poor fellow dropped a bag of apples and they must have rolled all the way to the bottom.

The view from the wall was magnificent. The scenery was beautiful, crowned by steep, green mountains. That people could build such a structure on such steep hills some 4,000 years ago seems unbelievable. According to legend, thousands of men died in the process and were buried under the wall.

The crowning event of our welcome in Beijing was a sumptuous banquet given by the Bureau of Foreign Affairs. The tables were loaded with a variety of exotic dishes of chicken, pork, squab, and octopus, along with fish we couldn't identify. They lacked the best—Loren's crispy Rock Creek catfish.

Many of the dishes were a mystery to us. Fruits and vegetables, breads and noodles, there was something for every palette. Here I got my first taste of plastic noodles, which were fine and almost transparent, and seemed to me to be tasteless. Later I learned that they were made of rice and potato water. But I never learned to like them.

Other tables were loaded with sweets of all kinds. But the most interesting were the 1,000-year-old eggs. They weren't actually 1,000 years old. They were duck eggs that had been buried in lime in the ground for 60 days, then dug up and relished as a pickled delicacy. This process gave them a cheeselike taste. Not too bad, but not good either. I'll take mine deviled! Now we know where green eggs and ham come from, I thought.

It was a glorious banquet with music and entertainment primarily by our own people. The Chinese delight in having their guests perform. We ended our "warmly welcoming" stay in Beijing on a happy and satisfied note, and looked anxiously toward going to our new home. After Beijing, life would never be the same again.

3

Riding the Iron Rooster

Tuesday morning came, and with it came Ann to take us to the train, China's famed Iron Rooster. This time she actually provided a taxi. If we thought she would be accompanying us on this 17-hour trip to Dalian across strange lands of eastern China, old Manchuria, we were sorely mistaken. She and her friend had other plans for the day. Fortunately, the young man was strong and willing to help us wrestle our luggage, which was the one blessing I could see about the whole situation. We had only begun to learn the reasoning of the Chinese mind. I don't think we ever really understood it.

Being "soft Americans" accustomed to checking through the luggage when traveling on public con-veyances, we assumed that the larger pieces of lug-gage would be checked through. The responsibility for handling this was Ann's. We had never imagined the amount of paperwork this simple process required.

We had arrived at the station with plenty of time to spare. However, being unused to the process of checking luggage, Ann struggled with the paperwork so long that we were in danger of missing the train. Finally we simply gave up and agreed to carry all of the luggage on board with us. And that was the beginning of what must have been a hilarious sight.

Actually, the train was pulling out. Everything had been moving at a snail's pace until then. I became agitated and fearful that we would miss boarding because we could not check our luggage. "Not to worry," we were told. Hearing this standard Chinese phrase for the first time did not really ease our minds. As a matter of fact, we soon learned that when we heard these words, it was time to start worrying.

"Forget checking the luggage," Loren said as he began hefting as many bags as he could carry. "We'll take them with us." We learned later this was what passengers did in China. No one checked luggage. No wonder Ann couldn't figure out how to do it.

There was just one problem with this. Our compartment was in the middle coach of the train, which had begun to move. Surely we were a funny sight as we all grabbed the heavy bags and ran to catch our coach, luggage flapping under our arms like the wings of scampering geese. Loren and I clambered aboard the train while Ann's friend hoisted bags to us through the train window. At last we had reason to give thanks for Ann's indiscretion. Without her friend, we may never have made it.

Safely on board, we breathed a sigh of relief, but only for a moment. There was a problem concerning the compartments Ann had booked for us. Looking at our tickets we discovered that we were in two different compartments. Evidently Ann had assumed that, being elderly and of the opposite sex, we would need to be placed in separate sleepers, no matter that we had slept together for over 40 years.

I had been placed with an elderly couple who could speak no more English than I could speak Chinese. They did not look happy. Loren, on the other hand, was sharing a compartment with a handsome young Japanese man. It just did not make sense to separate a husband and wife. Ann's sense of propriety was skewed.

But God worked through this situation. The young man was a Japanese student on his way to study at our university. And what's more, *he could speak English!* He and Loren quickly invited me to move in with them, and we spent a delightful morning getting acquainted with Takuma Sugimura. He had finished his degree at Tokyo University and would begin work on an advanced degree at Dongbei University. Ours was a friendship that would continue throughout our stay in China. But that was not the last of God's provisions for us that day.

About noon the train stopped at a small station and the gentleman boarding there came into our compartment. He was Professor Li, a professor of mathematics at our university. He proved to be a great blessing to us although we would not realize it until the next morning. I believe that he was another "angel of the Lord (who) encamps around those who fear him, and he delivers them" (Psalm 34:7 NIV). How wise God is. If Ann had been with us, we would not have been able to spend this precious time with these two fine people, our first friends in China. It was suddenly easy to forgive Ann her neglect.

Since we were on a "soft sleeper," we were able to get some sleep that night. Our arrangement, Loren on the top berth, me on the bottom, was one we continued to use in all our train travels in China. The next morning's event, though shocking, was one to which we finally became accustomed.

Early, before the sun was up, the stewardess came around and demanded our sheets and pillowcases. Apparently the stewardesses were responsible for having the linens put away before the train ended its run into Dalian. We never really got used to this practice of yanking the linens out from under us before daybreak. It resembled a magic act in which the magician whips a tablecloth from a table, leaving the dishes undisturbed. *We* were disturbed! We took a number of long train trips in China which can sometimes get to be a bit boring; sleeping a little longer in the mornings helps to use up a part of the day. But since we knew we would be arriving into Dalian soon, we were too excited to sleep this morning.

In spite of the sheet fiasco, the stewardesses were not too hard-hearted. Just before we arrived in Dalian, one young stewardess came into our compartment, closed the door, and pointed to my fingernails.

I got out my polish for her. She polished the nails on one of her hands, and I polished the other. I tried to give her the bottle of polish, but she refused. I did not know it then, but she could have been accused of theft with very dire consequences. She was already breaking the rules by being in our compartment with the door closed. She had an excited and furtive air about her. But she was lovely and sweet, and I could not help but have joy in what had happened, as insignificant as it was.

It was before sunup when we pulled into the beautiful city of Dalian. Our organization's director had told us we had received the plum assignment in China, as indeed we were soon to agree.

Dalian is the northernmost seaport city in China, looking east toward the Yellow Sea, and is one of the country's busiest seaports. On the southeast coast of Liaoning Province, which hangs down like a fat Chinese pigtail between the mainland and Korea, Dalian lies 200 miles directly east of Beijing as the crow flies. Famous for its beaches and resorts, its bay is dotted with small volcanic islands. It is beautiful!

Compared to most cities in China, Dalian is very modern and progressive, a place noted for business and industry. But more importantly to us, it is a place of learning, boasting 122 scientific research institutes and 12 colleges and universities. And we came to teach in one of them!

It's often dangerous to rely on first impressions, but it has always been a mystery to me why trains invariably arrive in the seediest part of town. If there are slums anywhere, the trains always seem to gravitate to them.

While Dalian had no slums, the late style of architecture left something to be desired. The buildings all looked gray in the soft light of morning, a color which permeated most of the city since a majority of the buildings were unpainted block or stucco and plaster.

We disembarked at the station which, although actually downtown, was deserted at this early morning hour. Professor Li and Takuma helped us unload our luggage through the train windows just as they had been loaded. We searched expectantly for some sort of a "warmly welcoming" committee, but Ann had failed to inform the local Foreign Affairs that we would be arriving, and there was no one there to meet us. Again she had left us stranded and to our own devices. It was then that we realized why the Lord had brought Professor Li across our path.

Realizing our dilemma, he asked us to wait in the soft-sleeper waiting room while he went to phone the school. But since school was not yet in session, everyone was on holiday, and there was actually no one available to meet us. Professor Li then did a very practical but dangerous thing. He unofficially procured a van parked at the station, loaded all of our luggage into it, and took us to our school's Foreign Experts Guesthouse.

Our "angel" had delivered us. We were home at last in Dalian.

China Sunrise

"I shall miss the rising of the sun," I thought,
Drinking in the morning beauty of my home.
"The path the moon makes on the lake at night
As it rises from Neosho's glistening foam."

But, oh, the wonder of the Chinese sky!
What a foolish thing that was for me to say!
I glory in the sun on Guan Ritai
And the brilliant path of moonlight on the bay.

The world, the whole of it, belongs to Him!
He made the sun to rise in China, too.
I've never seen a fairer autumn moon,
Nor waters at the sunrise quite so blue.

This is my Father's world, the whole of it,
A sacred honor gave He to these men.
For from the East He called those ancient ones
To worship at His crib in Bethlehem.

—Thelma Notley

4

Dongbei on the Hill

The manager of the Foreign Experts Guesthouse had not expected us so soon. Another couple, the teachers we were replacing, was still in our apartment and would not vacate it for a while. They seemed in no hurry to leave.

"Not to worry," said the manager. So of course we worried. Where would we lay our weary heads? Where could we finally unpack our bags? *Where was home?*

Home, though temporary, became an unoccupied top floor apartment assigned to another American teacher who had not yet arrived. Here we would stay until our own apartment was available. We were happy to be up where we could have a good view of Bo Hai Bay and its islands to our east. Both the living room and the bedroom were east rooms and had sliding glass patio doors opening out onto a small balcony. It was light and airy; and since the weather was still warm, we felt fortunate to have the coolest apartment in the building. To our surprise, we received oscillating fans to help move the humid August air.

Furnished in the Western style, the guesthouse apartments had carpeted floors, large overstuffed chairs with starched slipcovers and antimacassars on the backs and arms, and footstools. And best of all, end tables, complete with teacups and thermoses full of hot water for tea, sat beside the chairs. No Chinese living room would be complete without such a tea service. And because there was no kitchen in this apartment, it was the responsibility of the hotel kitchen to keep residents supplied with hot water.

These were the dog days of summer at home, and the weather here, hot and sultry, seemed comparable to what we had just left. At least in this way we felt not really so far away from home. One might only want to stay inside the cool rooms, look out on the sparkling bay, and collapse in the big chairs near the open doors. But not us. There was too much to see. Changing into the coolest clothes we could find, we started out to explore the deserted campus.

Being so near the ocean, we had not expected the dry, dusty paths and streets. The air held a strange antithesis. For all the humidity we felt, causing our clothing to cling to us in the sweltering heat, we also felt a dryness that caused the dust to rise up from our footsteps and clog our throats. What we had yet to learn was that China has very little ground cover and is almost barren. Grass is almost nonexistent. Even the slightest breeze whipped dust into our faces.

The Chinese government had recently instituted a new greening-up policy, reversing what Chairman Mao had decreed during the Cultural Revolution. He had earlier required the removal of all unproductive vegetation in order to use any arable land for food production. Now, trees were considered endangered species. Flower gardens began erupting everywhere. Even evergreen shrubs became things of beauty, marvels to behold. In the center of the city and all along the boulevards, clever hands had sculpted large evergreen shrubs into the images of animals like elephants and bears. Two large undulating dragons graced the fountain in Stalin Square.

Although the campus was deserted, we roamed over the entire complex, attempting to decipher the buildings in which we would be teaching. We easily discerned a very fine classroom building, and the dormitories were unmistakable. Also easy to identify was the administration building. And, of course, we soon discovered the campus store.

As a retired librarian, I was drawn to the beautiful library building. Although it was closed, as were all the other buildings, we stood like curious children with our faces pressed against the glass windows, peering into the marvelous "sanctuary." I yearned to be able to enter and have access to all the books. It didn't occur to me at the time that most of them were in Chinese. And, of course, we had never really learned to read Chinese.

Never mind.

The whole world wanted to learn to speak English, we reasoned, and that was why the Chinese government had brought us here. Surely there must be an ample supply of books in English. Our foolish American egos were about to take a tumble!

During our stroll around campus we encountered one of the teachers we had come to replace. Her husband had had problems with alcohol during their stay, with almost fatal results. They had developed a close association with some of the officials on the campus and had become drinking buddies. But this man's relationship with his Chinese friends came to a dreadful climax when, during a drinking bout, he came too close to the rails on the balcony and fell three floors to the hard ground below. His life had been spared, but most of the bones in his body had been broken. As a result, he had spent weeks in recuperation, both at the local hospital and in our apartment.

Although he was not yet fully recovered, the time had come for them to vacate the rooms and return to the States. Quite naturally, neither one of them was particularly glad to see us. It meant a definite end to their stay in China. We were there to push them out and take their places.

In later days when the school authorities evidenced great amounts of kindness and respect for us, we attributed much of it to the poor behavior of this couple. The school soon began to see the difference between our Christian lifestyle and that of others. They wanted to credit it to our age, but we felt they knew it was more basic than that. We wanted the Chinese to see, not us, but the love of God in us. That desire was uppermost in our hearts the entire time we were there. That was our earnest prayer.

The departing teacher was not the only young woman we ran into on the campus. The best day we'd had in China to that point was the day we ran into Rosanna.

Rosanna! What a name and what a person!

Rosanna, a teacher associated with our sponsoring organization, was young and vibrant, a vivacious addition to our new life. It was love at first sight!

She had taught at the university the year before, serving alongside an older woman teacher. Having finished college shortly before coming to China, she was hardly older than the students she taught. They loved her and identified with her. She had a way of reaching them that we older teachers did not have.

And she was funny!

"I hated it when I heard they were sending an *old* couple here," she informed us.

She could be great for the ego.

"Thanks," we laughed. "We love you too."

"Have you seen the library?" she asked.

There was something going on in that crazy head of hers. We didn't know her very well yet, but we could tell.

"What a question to ask a librarian," I countered indignantly. "I'm always interested in the library."

"If only she could get in," Loren laughed. "They have her locked out."

They were ganging up on me. They quickly learned to do that. They *loved* doing that! But sometimes it went the other way and Rosanna and I ganged up on Loren, or Loren and I took on Rosanna. It was always great fun. This was the day the fun began.

"I mean, have you seen *all* of the library building?" Rosanna persisted.

We were puzzled.

"What more is there to see?" we wanted to know.

That's what Rosanna was waiting for. She had whipped up our curiosity.

"Come and look."

The campus had been built on a hill, which dropped away on the far side of the library building. A retaining wall stood on the edge of a cliff which descended perhaps 50 feet to the street below. At the far corner of this building, next to the retaining wall, was a small stone enclosure with neither a gate nor a door. Within this small compound was a set of metal stairs leading from the wall down to the ground. There was no way to access them. To reach the top of the stairs, one would have to be a gymnast and leap the wall to land at the top of the stairs. Once upon the stairs, if one descended to the ground, there was no place to go. They were "the stairs from nowhere to nowhere," giving us the first glimpse of many things in China that seemed ridiculous and nonsensical to us. We were coming to realize that there was much about China and the Chinese mind we didn't understand.

5

Hai Shi Jiao

Learning how to change money in any country can be confusing. In China it sometimes seemed especially so. Street vendors in some of the country's interior often buttonhole tourists and foreigners with "Changee monee?" although this was not prevalent in Dalian.

Changing money was, in fact, almost a freelance occupation for some Chinese. The only time we really encountered it in Dalian was shortly after we had settled into our new apartment. We had opened a bank account with the Bank of China and had become acquainted with an ambitious young teller. A short time later when we were at supper in the hotel dining room, I was called to the telephone. It was our new friend. Why he called for me and not for Loren we never understood, unless he thought I might be a softer touch. He informed me that even though we could change money at the bank, he himself could get us a much higher rate of exchange.

"Everyone does it," he informed me.

There were several people in the lobby of the guesthouse when I took the call, and I was aware they all knew who was calling and why. It angered me that I was approached in such a manner. I was really put on the spot.

In a burst of indignation I informed him that I was aware that changing money on the black market was against the law. We were there as guests of the Chinese government and we would never do anything that was against the law. I asked him never to call me again.

I did not realize it then, but one of the listeners was Mr. Li, the head of the Communist Party on campus. Nor did I realize that, in my response, I was really being tested. We later believed that by my response he was evaluating our character.

In the past in America we had come to fear and distrust the Communists. Not knowing that I was being watched, I had no fear. But our Lord says, "When a man's ways please the Lord, he maketh even his enemies to be at peace with him" (Prov. 16:7 KJV). In the days to come this man, "our enemy," became one of our staunchest supporters and did things for us no one else could do. Though I was not fearful, our Lord is faithful. He always delivered us from the hand of the enemy.

We had already changed money at the bank; and since money of any kind begs to be spent, we went about spending it.

As soon as our apartment became available, we settled right in, but Loren immediately saw things we could do to upgrade our new home. Always the fix-it man, he wanted to shop for hand tools and electrical wire to make extension cords. We never really could seem to get past the mind-set of soft Americans. We needed our creature comforts.

Just east of the campus, about a 10-minute walk from the guesthouse, lies the neighborhood and market of Hai Shi Jiao, meaning "black rock." This thriving little community takes its name from the beautiful rock formations on the beach. Although it was decidedly Chinese, we felt comfortably at home there. It seemed to us to resemble some of the small rural communities where we had lived and worked.

We began our experience of shopping in the small sidewalk shops looking for dishes and tableware, pots and pans, and other items that soon turned our apartment into a home. The local merchants must have felt they had discovered a bonanza in their new customers because it was there that we purchased most of the things we needed. Eventually we bought wooden hangers and clothespins because we were not aware of any electric washers or dryers. Once, when purchasing a tea kettle, the merchant examined every kettle on her shelves and chose for us the one with the least dents and flaws. My prize purchase was a genuine Chinese meat cleaver which I have to this day.

The merchants loved to see us come and were kind. Understanding that we did not speak the language, they were courteous and helpful. Although we had learned how to change money, we could not estimate the value of things. When paying for the items we purchased, we simply held out the Chinese currency, which we did not yet understand, and let them take what we owed. They would then give us our change. I do not believe that we were ever cheated or shortchanged the whole time we were in China. We trusted the merchants and were never deceived.

The food market was especially interesting. No big name grocery stores here. But capitalism was beginning to creep into China through the independence of the farmers who were permitted to sell their garden produce in the open-air market.

Their vine- and tree-ripened fruits and vegetables rivaled any we could find in America and were brought fresh to the market each day. As a gardener, Loren loved to walk through the Hai Shi Jiao market appraising the vegetables and selecting the best. He never quibbled with the merchants, but he often bantered with the women before finally paying the asking price. They loved it. They became accustomed to us and actually looked forward to our visits.

Deposited directly on the gravel roads and sidewalks in the Hai Shi Jiao market area, we found great heaps of fruits and vegetables the farmers had brought into town. We had been warned that there was no cold storage for fresh foods through the winter months, so we would be wise to lay by as much of these goods as we could before they were gone. We carried home large quantities of both Irish and sweet potatoes, turnips and onions, and hung them in mesh bags on the hall tree in our entry hall. The hall tree became an ideal storage place for bags of fresh food.

One of the mainstays of the Chinese diet in winter is cabbage. We could usually buy it in autumn in the open market if the local farmers brought it in from their fields. Otherwise, we sometimes had trouble finding it. We did not attempt to preserve it as the Chinese did. The government distributes cabbage free to each household through a type of rationing system. Anything that was designated for us was automatically given to the cooks in the guesthouse, as the government presumed they were preparing our food.

In the autumn, truckloads of cabbages are brought in from the countryside and dumped on the roads and streets in most of the neighborhoods until they became almost impassable. There, each family receives its quota, and the housewives preserve them for winter. Since they have no way of canning or freezing them, they pickle them.

They first spread the cabbages out to mature and dry. We saw drying cabbages everywhere: on fences and rooftops, rock walls, balconies, and sidewalks. We saw them lined up in rows on the sidewalk before the front door. We even saw one row of cabbages on a sidewalk in downtown Dalian where every cabbage had been neatly tied with a red ribbon, giving them the appearance of young girls in brightly colored hair ribbons.

A visit in the home of a friend introduced us to the process of preserving the cabbages. After they are dried, the woman of the home takes them inside to be pickled. Each home contains a large stone jar that stands waist high into which the cabbages are carefully placed, row upon row, pressed down as tightly as possible, and covered with boiling water. A stone lid, placed securely over the cabbages and topped with a heavy rock, seals the cabbages and allows them to ripen. Salt is optional, I was told.

The Chinese must have been following this practice for generations, for all housewives seemed to do this in the fall. Pickled cabbage is a dietary staple, and to them it is delicious, although Loren and I tried it in our hotel dining room and did not care much for it. We preferred our cabbage fresh, and often had corned beef and cabbage for our Sunday dinner. There were no Chinese dishes which did not agree with us, although we liked some better than others. We had a tendency to lose weight at first, but soon began to fight the "battle of the bulge" again. In addition to corned beef and cabbage, we often enjoyed ham and beans on Sundays.

Sugar was another difficult item to find. It too was included in the government allotments to each household. The only way we were able to get sugar was to let our students know of our need. Soon we were inundated with "gift" parcels of sugar sent from the parents of our students.

The primary stove Chinese housewives use is a two-burner gas hot plate, one of which we also had in our apartment. They typically use this stove outdoors on the balcony because they love to stir-fry their foods in woks in very hot oil, and this allows them to do so without smoking up the apartment. Most of the homes we saw were furnished in this way, the balconies coated with the greasy smoke of years of cooking.

Chinese typically do not have ovens in their homes and therefore do not bake, instead buying their breads in neighborhood bakeries. They enjoy steam rolls and a type of flat bread similar to pita bread. The steam rolls are never browned and seemed very doughy and not quite done to me. Because they do not bake, they do not use flour, and we consequently had trouble finding it. It was not available in the markets or small grocery stores. Since flour is very much a requirement for American cooking, we needed to find where we could purchase it. It and beans were among our luckiest finds in China.

Amazingly, one day on the trolley ride to town, we passed an industrial building before whose open door was a spill of white on the ground which looked to us like flour.

Of course we investigated. We investigated everything!

And it *was* flour.

The small store was that of a government miller who supplied restaurants and hotels with baking supplies. Besides the flour, which they reluctantly allowed us to buy, we found all kinds of beans and grains. One interesting grain we did not recognize at first, but bought anyway, turned out to be sesame seeds. When I finally discovered what they were, I had a heyday making sesame seed cookies. They were the first I had ever made, and they were delicious.

We bought both pinto beans, which Loren loved, and navy beans, which I prefer. From then on we alternated the kind of beans we had for Sunday dinner. They were a welcome change from rice and noodles and we were never without ham and beans again. Strangely, we never heard of the Chinese housewives using them. They just didn't know what they were missing!

Eggs were in good supply and were available year-round. We located several "egg ladies" in the vicinity from whom we bought our eggs. One never buys a dozen eggs, but buys them by the kilo, usually about 30 eggs. Each egg lady had her own set of scales, as do most of the produce merchants. Their scales fascinated us, the kind we seldom saw at home, using pans and weights to measure. The most unusual had only one pan to hold the produce and hung balanced from a stick on a string. How the merchant could calculate the weight, we were never able to figure out.

The first eggs we bought were dirty, and half of them were bad. We soon learned which egg lady had fresh eggs, and we became faithful customers. Our favorite egg lady loved to see us come. All the other merchants around her knew that we "belonged" to her.

Eggs became a very important staple in our diet because good fresh meat was scarce. Once we bought a kilo of ground beef, but it was so full of gristle and sinew that we could not eat it. Later, in the downtown area of Dalian, we watched as butchers unloaded beef in front of their market. The great sides of meat were pulled off the open truck beds to land in the dirt and mud of the street. Because of

Chairman Mao's clean China policy, there were very few flies about to pollute the meat before it could be hauled inside. Nevertheless, that sight cured us forever of buying fresh beef in China.

We would not do as the Chinese did and buy fresh fish harvested from the bay. Having seen raw sewage running down the hill into the water of the bay, we were afraid of the fish, although we sometimes ordered seafood in the restaurants. I suspect the handling of pork was as unsanitary as the beef, though we never did see it. The Chinese love pork and eat it often. By the grace of God, we were never ill because of what we ate. However, we never ate anything without praying over it first. Many things happened to us, but nothing ever harmed us. We were under divine protection.

We did eat meat occasionally but, except for chicken, it was always canned. Our little campus store carried several kinds of canned meat; but since we couldn't read the labels, we had to do a good bit of experimenting to discover what the various cans held. Canned pork, with the picture of a pig on the label, became a staple for sandwiches. We could get good New Zealand corned beef from the Foreigner's Friendship Store downtown, which we usually reserved for Sunday dinner since it was expensive. Other cans of meat had labels picturing horses or dogs.

Dog meat is very popular in China. One never sees a dog running loose, for they are kept penned up, fattened, and used for food. We witnessed this once when we were taken on a sight-seeing trip in a resort area. Walking near the bathhouse, we came upon a pen of dogs being prepared for butchering. The only time I bought dog meat, it was so strong that I immediately carried it outside to the dumpster. Our

Chinese students were horrified when they learned I had thrown away "good meat," for they seldom had as much as they liked to eat. One of our greatest joys was to feed them.

Although food was often uppermost in our minds and we loved the market, we also enjoyed exploring the beach area. Situated here was a common bathhouse. Since clean, hot water was often in short supply, the Chinese did not usually have bathtubs in their homes. We never saw one on our frequent visits to the homes of our fellow teachers and students. The bathhouse was popular with the students who could afford to frequent it. Loren and I never did, for our guesthouse had a bathtub in every apartment, although hot water there was sometimes scarce.

Having never lived near the ocean and not being familiar with life on the beach, we were astonished at the foodstuffs the Chinese were able to glean from the bay. One unforgettable day, when we wandered down toward the water, we saw what seemed to us to be hordes of seaweed which had washed up on the sand. Actually, it was kelp, which the Chinese farm in the waters just offshore. Although it is not a familiar food to Midwestern Americans, we understood that it is nourishing, and a staple for the Chinese.

Needless to say, since the water was full of kelp as it washed ashore, very few students swam that day. But the beach was full of local people who had come to harvest what they could and take it home for their suppers.

It was in this area that we discovered a very fine restaurant. This was great for us because it was near the campus in a guesthouse near Xinghau Park. We began going there once a week for a midweek break with some of the other teachers and foreigners. Since it was something of a resort hotel, the food was much better than we could get in our own dining room.

We learned to eat with chopsticks before we left home. While in Dalian, we purchased lovely lacquered ones. Even though we had Western tableware in our apartment, we always used chopsticks when eating out. It was fun, and it made us feel that we were making a transition to live like the Chinese. We wanted to, "when in Rome, do as the Romans do."

6

Popcorn and Chicken Soup

Although we loved the local market in Hai Shi Jiao, we were fascinated with the sights of downtown Dalian. Family and friends at home may have worried for our safety, but the most danger we faced in Dalian was riding the public buses. While we were aware of the millions of people crowded into China, we still sometimes wondered if they didn't all want to ride the number 23 bus at the same time we did. It was almost like taking your life in your hands just to board that bus.

Having never lived in a large metropolitan area, I had never seen such buses and was amazed the first time I saw one. Two bus bodies are joined together at the center with a large round metal plate, which acts as a pivot and rotates, allowing the bus to bend to turn corners.

The large population, combined with few privately owned vehicles, means that most Chinese ride the bus. The crowds that queue up to board the buses are many times greater than the capacity of the bus; therefore, they push and shove, sometimes violently, to get onboard. It is not unusual for bus drivers to slam the door in the faces of the people trying to crowd in. Once we saw a shoving match turn into a fistfight when it moved onto the bus. The driver could not close the doors until some of the passengers had pushed the fighters off.

At first, we timidly held back. But because we were white-haired foreigners, the Chinese people often deferred to us and allowed us to board unchallenged. I was usually offered a seat even though many were already standing. This courtesy gradually diminished with time as the people in our area became accustomed to us and began to treat us as one of their own. Then they began to expect us to vie for a seat like everyone else, although they continued to treat us courteously.

Out of desperation, for it was too far to walk to town, we learned to push our way onto the buses. I became so used to this practice that the first time we traveled to Hong Kong, where the crowds were smaller and the fine subway system is sufficient to carry everyone comfortably, I pushed my way onto a car. The passengers boarding with me stepped back, giving me shocked looks. Imagine my embarrassment when I realized I had automatically behaved in the same manner that had once startled me in China. It was a lesson in courtesy I would never forget.

The trolley offered the easiest way to travel downtown. Since it was more expensive and usually less crowded, people were a little friendlier and often felt freer to speak to us. We loved trying to converse with them. It was easiest when there were children aboard who were fascinated by the "old foreigners." Since English was a required language in school, some of the children understood a little of what we said. They seemed especially drawn to Loren. Although his face and demeanor was that of a younger man, his white hair rendered him kind and reassuring; and they seemed not to be afraid of him. He was like their own dear grandfathers.

Before leaving Tulsa we had purchased T-shirts and heavy fleece warm-up suits with words printed on them that said, in Chinese, *I Love China.* This particular form of the Chinese word for love meant a very deep and passionate love. It usually triggered comments. We were often asked, "Do you know what your shirt says?"

What an opening!

We would respond affirmatively, reassure them that we did love China, and explain that that was the reason we had come.

To our students, this was amazing because life in China can sometimes be hard. Many of our students dreamed of going to America. For Americans to come for the love of China was almost beyond their comprehension. Although it would come, it was not yet time to tell them that it was not our love, but God's, that had brought us here.

Saturday was the Foreign Experts official shopping day. On that day, the school provided a van and driver to take us downtown for the day, delivering us to the central part of the city where they picked us up late in the afternoon, laden with purchases, treasures, and food. Weary and foot sore, we were happy with our day out. Shopping in Dalian never resembled shopping at home. No Wal-Marts here!

We explored. We found department stores, sidewalk shops, restaurants, and bakeries. We even found a great open-air farmers market! We learned what each of the large department stores offered. Mostly, we just enjoyed looking at what they offered to the Chinese people.

Our favorite store was the Foreigner's Friendship Store, patronized mostly by foreigners who had foreign exchange certificates (FEC) to spend. Most Chinese people do not have this special currency and instead use only the regular Chinese currency, the yuan. It had no value on the international exchange market and seemed like play money to us. The FEC could be exchanged internationally. We had both it and yuan. Although we were paid in yuan, we exchanged the American dollars we brought with us for FEC, which we could eventually change back to dollars when we were ready to leave China.

At noon on our Saturday trips we would gather at the New International Hotel restaurant where we would eat our one Western meal of the week. We drank American coffee and stuffed ourselves with hot rolls and butter, hamburgers, and french fries. I often gorged on great fried shrimp, cooked American-style.

Because the chef at this hotel was French, we sampled foods from different parts of the world every week. We seemed to be walking through our culture shock with food. Soon, however, we became accustomed to good Chinese food and preferred it. Patronizing the better Chinese restaurants taught us what good Chinese food really is.

The Friendship Store carried some foods, as well as goods, of a finer quality than we could find in the other stores. Since Friendship Stores catered to foreigners, they would accept only FEC. Many of the souvenirs and gifts we brought back were purchased there. This was one of the rare places where we could get Coca-Cola. And here we could get American coffee and the New Zealand corned beef that turned Sunday dinner into a Sabbath feast. But we missed our popcorn.

Through the years, one of our favorite family pastimes had been devouring popcorn as we watched television in the evenings. This was usually Loren's treat for the family, especially when the children were small and all were still at home. And this was no microwave popcorn. The microwave was still floating around in some inventor's dream world and had not been invented yet; or at least, we didn't know about it. Loren's popcorn was better than any microwave popcorn I have ever found.

Loren had tried several kinds of popcorn poppers. Most were failures. Either the corn didn't pop or it burned. We even owned a wire basket popper we held over the coals in the fireplace. It didn't work very well. Loren's method was the best. He discovered my pressure cooker.

He melted a little butter or shortening in the hot pan, poured just enough corn into the pan to cover the bottom, and put the lid on tightly without the pressure gauge. Placing the pan over a hot fire, he shook it gently as the corn popped. It came out perfect! We all thought he was the greatest popcorn popper in the world.

There was one kind of popcorn popper, though, that he had never used—the Chinese popcorn popper. We only saw it used once, in the dormitory yard across the street from our building.

It was a rather miserable winter day when we heard what sounded to us like gunfire. Rushing out to see what was happening, we saw a little man sitting on the ground with what looked like an old inner tube, which he was holding over a small fire.

Students had gathered around him, muffled up against the biting north wind, watching him with anticipation. After a few moments we understood the source of the "gunshot."

It wasn't a gunshot at all, but the explosion of popcorn in his inner tube popcorn popper. Holding the heavy, rubber bag over a heat source such as canned and liquid fuel, he was able to heat all the kernels at the same moment and all exploded simultaneously—no tedious shaking, no unpopped kernels left in the bottom.

The students eagerly retrieved their order of the hot popcorn and rushed back into the warmth of the dormitory while the popcorn man patiently prepared to pop another batch. Loren had finally found someone whose process was more unique than his. We wondered if the popcorn tasted like rubber. We never found out.

Since Loren loved popcorn so, we had managed to bring a small package of it with us in our bags. A friend, who had also taught in China, had popped corn in her wok. After our arrival, we anticipated the larger amount of popcorn that would come in our trunk.

At first we tried using the wok to pop corn. It worked, but not very well. The oil we used we purchased from our guesthouse cooks to use in our own kitchen. Once someone sold us chicken fat, which I returned immediately when I discovered what it was.

The oil we normally used was a poor quality of soybean oil, probably not refined very well. Its strong taste did nothing to complement the popcorn. Loren had always used butter or vegetable shortening, but we could find neither of these in China.

Never mind! It was popcorn.

Imagine our delight when on one of our rambling trips through the department stores downtown, we found pressure cookers exactly like the one we had left at home. Chinese housewives use pressure cookers to cook rice. Forever after, we used ours to make popcorn, and to cook beans, corned beef, and cabbage. Of course it was not the same brand as the one we used at home, but what did that matter? It could pop corn!

I bought Loren one for his birthday.

♦

Loren was a collector. He collected all sorts of things like nuts and bolts, old door and bathroom fixtures, and things I could never imagine needing. We built a house using many of the throwaways he had collected and thereby saved ourselves a good deal of money. He collected people, too.

In most of our travels, he usually came across someone he knew. If he didn't know them, it was not long before he did. He collected lovely people in China.

The first one was Professor Yao, brother of the author of *Life and Death in China,* the last book we read before leaving home. They had met on campus when Loren was trying to find a barber. The one Professor Yao recommended just happened to be the brother of the president of the university. Professor Yao told Loren that if he got a really short haircut, it would make him handsome. Later he came to see how the haircut had turned out.

"I'm mad about the haircut," Loren told him.

Professor Yao was crestfallen.

"Why?" he wanted to know.

"Because it didn't make me handsome," Loren laughed.

Professor Yao just roared. He was so grand.

He was so fine and so funny.

He came for tea.

He came for the party.

We became great friends.

We left many friends behind in China. Someday we hope to see them all again.

Loren's birthday was September 3 and usually fell during the first week of school at home. As headmaster of a private Christian school, his faculty and staff catered to him. It was not unusual for him to be treated to several parties including the family celebration I always gave him. But we were in China. Where would I get a cake and who would come to his party?

I had planned ahead. I *usually* plan ahead.

Crammed in with all the necessary things in our suitcases, I had managed to hide a cake mix, frosting, pan, and candles.

But what was I to do for an oven?

With faith in my heart and a prayer on my lips, I mixed my cake and took it down to the hotel kitchen. Would they bake the cake for me? I asked.

They would on one condition— that I give them the pan. Gladly I agreed. It was one of the throwaway pans anyway, a small price to pay for having a cake. I had even brought trick candles for the cake.

But, who would come to the party? Our fellow teachers, of course. And Professor Yao. Some of the Chinese had never seen trick candles. When Loren tried to blow them out, they would burst into flame again. Our guests laughed until the tears ran. It made for a very successful party, no matter that we were so far from home.

We had several special guests besides Professor Yao, including a couple of teachers from the Institute of Industry Management in Chongqing, which Americans know as Chunking. They were on a sight-seeing trip through eastern China, which was actually a scouting trip to find new teachers for their school. They wanted us.

Loren's new popcorn pan was not all we found in our wanderings downtown. Although shopping there was somewhat tiring, it was also fun. We must have looked like American hippies when we shopped downtown, carrying backpacks we quickly filled. We also bought mesh shopping bags, soon bulging with our purchases, most of which were food.

A favorite experience was shopping in the large open-air farmers market. Although it was open, it was covered with a large canopy. The offerings, rows of both vegetables and fowl, were displayed on long tables. We felt like explorers as we went down the aisles, seeing what unusual things we could find.

And find strange things we did: unusual vegetables, exotic gleanings from the ocean, and chicken, one of the most amusing offerings. Several times we bought fresh chicken there. It seemed the farm wives brought chickens into town from the country each day, displaying them on tables they stood behind.

Having lived in the country as a girl where we raised our own chickens, I could usually tell if a chicken was fresh or not. This I did by sniffing the bird. If it was old, its odor was usually a dead give-away. We had good luck choosing our chickens. We never got a bad one.

These Chinese chickens, however, seemed to have a life after death. Once we walked past some pretty poor birds looking for a fresh one. As Loren passed one sad, dark, shriveled specimen, the little chicken lady, frantic at seeing potential foreign customers getting away, grabbed her little "blue bird" and began slapping him on the breast as if to bring some color and life back into him.

It was hard not to laugh.

Of course, we didn't buy.

I remembered what our daughter Kathy had said to me when I tried to revive some house plants.

50

"Mother," she laughed, "don't you know you can't resurrect the dead?"

Apparently this woman didn't know that.

The chickens always came whole, including the head and "scratchers." We learned that the head is the prize piece of the chicken, for the Chinese love to pick out the brains. A frozen bird we bought once must have been a sideshow freak, for when we thawed him out we discovered that he had three heads and no liver or gizzard. (Just three heads!) Some poor housewife got a headless chicken with our liver and gizzard. How cheated she must have felt.

We had the ultimate chicken experience when we were invited to dinner at the home of friends. It was not a dinner. It was a banquet! The preparations were a part of the festivities. They did a good deal of their cooking in steam cookers, deep fryers, and woks right at the table.

The husband, a professor at our university, was making my favorite Chinese food, *jiaozi*, which are small meat or vegetables dumplings, either boiled or fried. I loved to eat them along with buds of raw garlic and could happily have passed up the rest of the meal for the jiaozi.

A small portion of filling is placed in the center of a circle of dough. Then the dough is folded over, edges sealed, and the dumpling is cooked in boiling water. The professor saw my interest and tried to teach me how to make them. Folding the dough seemed much like folding a diaper and, as we had four children, I should have been an expert. But I wasn't. I was all thumbs at first. When I made a mistake in the maneuver of folding the dumpling, he would gently slap my hand, take it from me, and do it right.

I did only a few to his satisfaction. Although he seemed a perfectionist about his creations, they all tasted the same in the end, perfect (and delicious)!

Of course, there was a great steaming kettle of noodles, wonderful soup, vegetables, and fluffy steamed rice. But the most memorable dish of the evening was fried chicken. As it is at home, it was seasoned, floured (where did she get the flour?), and dropped piece by piece into deep, hot fat. When they were done, the lovely hostess took them up and put select pieces on each plate.

That was when I discovered that I was the guest of honor. When I bit into mine I encountered something hard. I looked, and something was looking back at me.

It was the eye of the chicken!

I had been given the prize piece, the head! Laughing at my dismay as I laid the unwelcome head aside, my hostess graciously gave me another piece. It was an honor that was never bestowed on me again, to my great relief.

We enjoyed the chickens.

We enjoyed the jiaozi.

We were falling in love with China.

7

Between the Garden and the Gate

In the early fall we noticed that workmen were doing something between our building and the faculty apartment building behind us. Until now it had been a weed patch full of rocks and briers. Like most of the yard, it was not level and was very unsightly. It looked as though nothing could ever grow there. But we soon suspected that the workmen were preparing to make a small garden or park.

Their first task was to remove the weeds and level the rocky ground as much as possible. We were intrigued with what came next. With chalk, they laid out lines in a grid pattern, interwoven with a serpentine ditch they filled with rock. Soon they began to plant small trees following the serpentine pattern, which eventually became a walk. By spring flowers and small benches appeared under the trees, and what had once been an eyesore had become a thing of beauty.

Near the guesthouse on campus was a preschool for children of faculty and staff. Because it stood next to a building where Loren taught every morning, he soon became friends with the tiny children.

Few parents in China use diapers. Instead, babies' clothing has "split seats," which allow the children to relieve themselves through an opening in the back of their trousers. Both boys and girls who have not yet had toilet training wear this type of pant.

When the weather turned colder, we noticed that all the little children were well bundled up, appearing healthy and superbly happy. Their brightly-colored warm coats and snowsuits matched their ruddy cheeks as they came in from the cold. The only tears we saw were the normal tears of a child who has not gotten his way about something.

Because of China's one-child rule, most children have one set of parents and two sets of grandparents to dote on them. Often the government transfers a child's parents to separate cities for work, while the child stays with grandparents who may vie for his affection and try to outdo each other in catering to him. We wondered if this present generation of children would become a problem to the government in the future because they have been so catered to. But to us they seemed just like other children the world over. They love to be loved and pampered.

Loren not only loved to talk to the children, he also "collected" parents who came to know and trust him around their children. One day we encountered a young mother who was wearing an ivory pendant around her neck. It was of an Oriental woman. When we asked her about it, she held her hands up in an attitude of prayer. She was wearing her god. Just that morning Loren and I had read about the ox yoke Jeremiah had worn at God's command. When we saw the pendant, we thought of Jeremiah and wondered what invisible yokes we may have been carrying about our own necks.

54

The young children of the preschool were not the only little ones we came to know. We had the distinct honor of being named honorary grandparents to a new baby boy. A friend in Tulsa had asked us to take a gift to a young couple living in Dalian. They would be easy for us to find, she said, because they were both teachers. Unfortunately, when we tried to contact them, we had no luck. It was some time before we heard from them. The reason? They were on maternity leave. They had just had a baby boy.

At length they brought the baby to see us. Although they could speak no English, we had a lovely time cooing over the baby and taking pictures of Long Long. They asked us to be his honorary American grandparents. We never saw them again, but treasure the pictures of our Chinese grandson and the memory of the meeting of like minds. Teachers seem to be the same the world over.

Another couple we befriended served on the faculty of our university. A brilliant woman, Vera was revered as the best teacher in the English department. We became acquainted with John soon after he returned from study abroad. He had been gone for several years and Vera had been anxiously waiting for his return, which seemed natural to us. But it was not necessarily because she missed him.

Vera had been accepted for advanced studies in Edinburgh, Scotland. But according to China's policy, only one member of a married couple could leave the country at a time. The government, believing that the absent spouse would always return to the family, feared that couples who left together might be tempted to leave permanently, thereby depleting the country of one of its greatest resources, its intelligentsia. Vera could not go until John returned. While she had been expecting him all fall, he only reluctantly returned shortly before Christmas.

We liked John immediately. An impressive young man, he was mild-mannered, friendly, and highly intelligent. He and their 5-year-old daughter would live with his parents for 3 years, waiting at home until Vera returned just as she had waited for him.

Such instances of parents leading separate lives while grandparents care for the children is not unusual in China. We wondered what this did to the marriages. Either they are very strong to survive such separations, or they were marriages in name only. Sadly, the divorce rate in China is quite high. For example, there were over 1 million divorces in 1996 alone.

Young children and their parents were not the only people with whom we developed special relationships. Once, when the Department of Foreign Affairs took us on an outing to the scenic areas around Dalian, the elderly parents of one of the officials accompanied us. A lovely couple, they were a good deal older than we were; but as our hair was white, theirs was glistening black. Chinese people's hair does not usually turn gray until very late in life. It was one of the mysteries we never figured out.

We spent the day with the elderly Chinese couple at our side. They could not speak English, but we did not really need words to convey friendship. Though he did not need them, Loren enjoyed collecting canes and had purchased an ornate one in Anshan. Loren gave the old man his cane; and before the day was over the woman and I were walking arm in arm. When they left the bus at the end of the day, we watched them until they were out of sight, holding hands as he jauntily swung the cane, catching the attention of everyone who passed by.

If Loren loved the little preschoolers, I loved the elementary school children whose laughter we could hear so clearly. Located very near the guesthouse, this elementary school was on the next level down just below the campus. On our frequent trips to Hai Shi Jiao or to catch the downtown bus, we often walked through the schoolyard. As in schoolyards the world over during recess or the lunch hour, it teemed with children in brightly colored clothing laughing and playing at their games, calling out something we did not understand.

One day my friend Xiuzhen and I were on our way to the market when we were surrounded by shouting, laughing youngsters.

"Do you understand what they are saying?" she asked.

They were speaking Chinese, so of course I didn't. A little embarrassed, I shook my head as they swarmed about us.

"They are saying 'Ni hao nana' ("Hello, Grandmother')," laughed Xiuzhen.

Ever after, when we crossed the schoolyard to the shouts of the children, Loren and I quickly responded with "Ni hao," to the children's delight.

One aspect of the elementary schoolyard forever baffled and delighted us. Perhaps it was another case of a "Chinese fire drill."

Concrete gateposts on the road led from the campus to the elementary schoolyard. One day we noticed that workers were chipping holes in the posts. We watched as they hung two metal gates, which could be closed and locked at night against motor vehicles. Inside one gate was a smaller gate through which pedestrians could walk. But the large double gate had no center support. It had to be hung high enough to prevent it from dragging on the ground, but in doing so, the pedestrian gate was too high to be of much use to the children who could never navigate it. One morning, we noticed that the gate was gone and the holes in the gatepost were cemented back into place.

The planning which should have gone before was never done and the project had failed.

8

Sir, We Would See Jesus

"Come spend the coin of love I give," He says,
"And with My grace, buy China for My own.
Inherit all the uttermost parts of earth.
Your life of joy in me has just begun."
—Thelma Notley

Just before our departure to China, God put the final seal of His Word on our mission.

A group of beautiful young women from Tulsa had come to our lake home to minister to us. They showered us with His love. They laid hands on us and prayed for us. They anointed us with oil. They washed our feet and blessed us.

Then they commissioned us with His promise: "Ask of me, and I shall give thee the heathen for thine inheritance, and the uttermost parts of the earth for thy possession."

"Your life of joy in Him has just begun," Christy said.

We would go, and He would bless it. We never doubted. He would be with us all the way.

♦

We had been in China for a month. Each day we prayed, "Lord, let them see Jesus in us today." We had come to teach our students how to speak English, but it was our heart's desire that we would be able to demonstrate the love of Christ to them through our actions and attitudes.

English Corner, a weekly gathering of students and teachers in an open-air court on campus, provided students with opportunities to practice their English and converse with their teachers. They often entertained with songs and dances. More importantly, they could ask questions, any questions, about life in America.

Some of their questions were political. Whom would we vote for in the upcoming American presidential election? They were interested to know that even though we were in China, we could still vote by absentee ballot and that our votes would count. It seemed that most of China had an affinity for George Bush because he had been America's ambassador to China years before. They knew him, liked him, and trusted him. When he won the election, our students' reaction was "We won!" as if he were their candidate too. We felt the same affinity with them when a Chinese girl won the diving competition in the Olympics. "We won!"

Although China is not a democracy, the young people desperately desire a voice in their lives, their government, and their country. Tiananmen Square was later proof of that.

Our students were nosy.

Why had we come to China to teach? Was the Chinese government paying us a fabulous salary?

"We quit better paying jobs in America to come to China," Loren told them.

To live in America was a dream to most of them. For us to leave our comfortable lives and come to their country was unbelievable. They shook their heads in wonder when we told them, "We love China." It was a love they simply did not understand.

They were concerned about the backward state of China. The country's emphasis on education was leaving its mark.

"Do you think education will solve China's problems?" they asked.

"Education and knowledge alone are not enough," Loren explained. "With them must come wisdom. We believe that 'the fear of the Lord is the beginning of knowledge: but fools despise wisdom and instruction' (Prov. 1:7 KJV). This is what the Bible teaches us." A door seemed to be opening.

But they had no Bibles, nor any knowledge of the Proverbs. What we could not tell them yet was that it was not our love, but God's love that had brought us here.

We were beginning to adjust to life on campus. The freshmen, both men and women, did not come at the beginning of the semester but instead received their military training before they began classes. The upperclassmen, however, were already hard at work. Living in the dorms, they were awakened each morning with reveille played over the campus loudspeaker, which was also used to mark the different times of day with music. Often it was Western classical music. Beethoven seemed to be a favorite. Occasionally it was Western popular music from the 1940s and 1950s. On rare occasions the music was Chinese classical. All of it was harmonic and pleasing.

But the most exciting music proved to be a great blessing to me.

During the first week of school I lost my voice. Perhaps it was due to a cold, the change in climate, or an allergic reaction to the dust in the air. Or perhaps it was because I was not accustomed to lecturing without a sound system to a class of 100 students. I believed I had simply strained my voice, but Loren became anxious.

"I'm taking you home," he declared.

How could he? I wasn't sick! It was just another ploy of Old Slew Foot.

Admonished by the head of the English department to stay in bed, I lay contentedly under the shimmering gauze mosquito netting that hung like morning mist about my bed and listened to the sounds of life around me. I could hear the murmuring voices of the workmen talking in the garden below and the sweet laughter of the children in the schoolyard. The breakers whispered softly as they lapped the beach. I was enveloped in a deep sense of peace when the noon speaker came on.

Across the campus, over the city of Dalian, and out to sea flowed the precious strains of "Amazing Grace." I knew it was a benediction and a confirmation that we were where we were supposed to be, in the center of His perfect will.

We were settling into our new lifestyle when we were notified that the freighter carrying our trunk was in port. It had already been there for three weeks and would soon be sailing on to Greece.

We had asked regularly concerning the arrival of the trunk and had been told we would be notified when the ship arrived. We were "not to worry."

But the *Aigianis* had docked on August 10, even before we had arrived in China. It had been unloading for a month. Not until September 9 were we notified that it was in port and we could get our trunk.

"Three weeks! And we've been having rice gruel, pickles, and peanuts for breakfast in the guesthouse dining room!" we exclaimed.

But we were excited.

"Foreign Affairs has ordered a vehicle for tomorrow," Loren said.

But when tomorrow arrived, so did a van too small to accommodate our large trunk.

"We ordered a truck," he stated flatly.

"The order just says 'vehicle,'" replied the Chinese driver with a shrug. *These Americans are so unreasonable*, we sensed he was thinking. And he went back to the motor pool.

"Tomorrow," the Foreign Affairs director promised again.

But the next day while Loren sat patiently in the director's office, no truck arrived.

"Not to worry," he was told. "This is just the way it is in China. The request was too late for today. Come back tomorrow."

"But you promised," was on the tip of his tongue. To rebuke the official for a broken promise seemed justifiable, and natural. But we were there to demonstrate a new nature, that of the children of a patient and long-suffering Father. What had the Greek seekers said to Philip? "Sir, we would see Jesus" (John 12:21 KJV).

So Loren sat patiently and waited for the promised truck to arrive.

And finally it did.

Loren went with the driver to the dock, only to return empty-handed. "It's raining, and the stevedores don't work in the rain," the burly customs official told him. "We close at noon anyway. Come back tomorrow."

But the ship was due to sail at high tide the next morning. I had visions of the old trunk sailing serenely on to Greece with my precious electric blanket tucked securely inside.

By now the Foreign Affairs director was becoming uneasy because of the patient man who, day after day, sat quietly in the office waiting for the promised truck. When Loren's patience began to ebb and the tips of his ears began to turn red in frustration, the words of the Greek seekers came gently to his mind again.

"Sir, we would see Jesus."

Then the calmness of spirit that had controlled him so well would return.

On Friday a flatbed truck arrived. Faithful to the end, but with little hope of success, Loren climbed aboard, returning in triumph a short time later. With him was the trunk, battered and dented, but safe on China's soil at last.

The students who were waiting expectantly with us helped Loren haul the trunk into the lobby of the guesthouse. Since it was too heavy to carry up three flights of stairs to our apartment, we decided to open it there.

We unlocked the wonderful old trunk with all its treasures. Our friends had not believed us when we had told them all that it contained. What a celebration we would have with them over what they had begun to call the "magic trunk." There would be pancakes with our ham and eggs for Sunday brunch. What a wonderful taste of home!

Our friends and students stood around us as we unpacked our precious goods—Loren's oatmeal and popcorn; my Autoharp; and that wonderful, warm electric blanket. Everything stayed as it had been packed. Everything remained intact, including Loren's faithful witness to the unspoken request, "Sir, we would see Jesus."[1]

---

[1]Thelma A. Notley, "Sir, We Would See Jesus," *Confident Living,* February 1993.

9

The Three-Self Church

If Saturdays were the teachers' day to howl, Sundays became a day of rest. We had been told that we would not be able to attend the local church services. The Catholic Church in town seemed to be very poorly attended. China's long-standing Protestant Church was labeled the Three-Self Church: self-governing, self-supporting, and self-propagating. A survivor of the Cultural Revolution, it was again ministering to the body of Christ in Dalian.

Nevertheless, one day shortly after we arrived, a visitor who was a professor at neighboring university, invited us to accompany him to church the following Sunday. Eager and excited, we accepted his invitation. When the day arrived we rode downtown with him on the trolley, along with our fellow teacher.

We arrived late at the church and, although the services had started, the choir was still rehearsing their special music. Imagine how our hearts leapt for joy when we walked into the churchyard to the strains of "Revive Us Again." We felt at home. It was another confirmation that we were in the center of God's will.

The announcements and the message were in Chinese, of course, so we could not understand them. During the sermon, our professor friend informed us of the Scripture passages, and we read along in English as they read in Chinese.

As sweet as that was, sweeter still was the music. Every hymn was familiar to us. Those around us seemed delighted to hear us sing with them, not in the same language, but with the same Spirit. Christ truly is Lord and Savior of all the nations.

Because our sponsoring organization recommended caution in attending local worship services, we decided to be prudent, although we were not afraid. More important to us than exercising our freedom was not endangering the future liberty to witness to our students. They were why we had come, and we would not jeopardize that calling. If attending church openly became a stumbling block to our ability to witness, we would not go.

So we spent our Sundays quietly at home with our fellow teachers. We all loved to sing, so praise and worship became an important part of our time together. We shared responsibility for leading Bible study. But our prayertime was the backbone of our worship. Without prayer, I doubt that we could have accomplished much in China.

Sunday meant Sunday dinner, too. And since it was our largest home-cooked meal of the week, we enjoyed it with our friends. We alternated ham and beans with corned beef and cabbage. At times we enjoyed homemade banana bread or cinnamon rolls from the local bakery. We never did without, and we never went hungry.

Loren and I enjoyed the quiet, restful Sunday afternoons. Although we had a TV, all the programs were in Chinese and we were at a loss to understand them. Consequently, our set was unplugged and stored out of the way, under one of the desks. The only time we used it was to watch the Olympic games, which needed no language. And occasionally, students would ask if they could come and watch an American show which was being beamed into China with Chinese subtitles.

Sunday afternoons also offered plenty of time for recreational reading. Avid readers, we had brought a number of books with us, primarily biographies of great people of faith. We loved to read about missionaries, and we were also fans of James Michener. We came loaded with biographies, fictionalized histories, and geographers of America, as well as many other countries of the world. Even in China, we were armchair travelers.

Although we never again attended the regular church services in Dalian, we went there one more time at the request of our students, this time to see the church's Christmas program.

We did not know it at first, but it had required a good deal of maneuvering to get us "tickets." At home, we often had to persuade family and friends to come to the church's Christmas pageants. Not in China. On this particular occasion, we seemed to be the last to arrive. The church was packed and people were standing around the walls. Oddly enough, one bench near the front was vacant. It had been reserved for us!

As in the other service, this one seemed strangely familiar. The choir filed out, wearing choir robes much like those in our little church at home. And they began to sing. It was a Christmas cantata!

Scripture recitations of the Christmas story were interspersed with the carols we knew and loved. I was convinced that if we could have seen our church at home, the two services would have been identical. We were enveloped with warmth that belied the bitterly cold night outside. The love of God overflowed in that little Chinese church.

Not all was spiritual, however. As at home, there was a fat and squatty cedar Christmas tree decorated with popcorn, paper chains, lights, and even a star on top. Under the tree, to the children's delight, were tantalizing packages, one for each child in the church.

"I feel like I'm back at Falfa," Loren mused, as memories of Christmas in a little country church in the Kiamichi Valley came rushing in. But that was not all. A Santa, complete with a pack on his back, handed out the children's gifts after the choir had finished its program.

Then he did something I believe would be appropriate at any Christmas celebration. He gave gifts to the congregation, but not to everyone. There was a requirement in order to get a gift: knowledge of the Scriptures. We had a question-and-answer session! As Santa read questions from his Santa list, hands shot up all over the building. The first person with a hand up received the chance to answer a question from the Bible. If the answer was correct, he or she received a gift from Santa's pack.

The students who had brought us sat on either side of us and interpreted the questions. Veronica, my sweet student, would whisper each question in my ear, to which I would whisper back the answer. After several times of this give-and-take, she turned to me with wonder in her eyes and paid me a great compliment.

"You know the whole Bible, don't you?" she asked with amazement. Would that I did! I was her beloved teacher, and she was impressed enough to want to know more about the Bible herself. But the best part of the program was yet to come.

We had already learned that the Chinese love for their guests to entertain them. So those of us who were guests were asked to sing.

First to respond was an old Japanese gentleman. He had been a part of the occupying Japanese army during World War II. But as a Christian, he had attended the church during the war. This was something of a homecoming for him after nearly 50 years, and he happily ascended the podium and sang a carol in Japanese. Next to sing was a handsome young man from the Congo, an exchange student at the Marine College. With his beautiful tenor voice, he lifted up our hearts with his rendition of "To God Be the Glory." I have never heard it sung more gloriously.

At last we were asked to sing. Our voices had grown old and had a tendency to crack. Although we had sung in our own church choirs for many years, we were past the time when we could perform, even as a duet. But in China we had to learn to do it. Nervously, we climbed the stairs and stood behind the pulpit. At the piano ready to accompany us was one of my students, Charles, who had been one responsible for inviting us. Whispering, Loren and I discussed what we should sing. All the carols had been covered; and besides, we knew no songs in Chinese.

"Sing 'O Holy Night,'" Charles suggested.

We were stunned. Although it is one of the most beautiful Christmas songs ever written, he could not have requested a more difficult one. Praying for guidance, the answer seemed obvious.

There was only one song on which we could harmonize.

"Amazing Grace," I said, as I turned to Charles. The good pianist that he was, he began to play, and we began to sing.

Suddenly, it seemed that the glory of the Lord filled the building. The people began to smile. Then they began to weep. We motioned for them to join us.

If I never before understood the oneness of the body of Christ, I understood it that night. By the time we had reached the last verse, the people were standing. And they were singing with us as tears poured down all our faces.

When we've been there ten thousand years,
Bright shining as the sun,
We've no less days to sing God's praise
Than when we first begun!

It rang out in Chinese and English and Japanese.

He was there with us and all the languages were the same to Him.

Someday we shall do that again, as we stand before His throne!

10

Opening Doors

China's teachers employ a much different teaching style than most American teachers. In China, the teacher or professor usually enters the classroom after all the students are seated quietly and the monitor has checked the attendance. The teacher then mounts the podium, which is elevated several feet above the students, from which he lectures formally. There is little or no discussion. He then departs, leaving his students to work through the lessons on their own.

Much of their learning is by rote memory from textbooks. It was not unusual as we walked to class to pass through groups of students reciting aloud their lessons for the day. Scattered about the schoolyard, alone with their studies, their voices hummed around us as they repeated aloud the things they must remember. If our students ever did this over our assignments, we were not aware of it. We didn't require memorization. We wanted them to internalize what they learned and not simply give lip service to it.

Our classes were held in two buildings. Most of Loren's classes were in the large and spacious classroom building, while mine were in an older, darker building. This particular building must have had a history, for there were guards stationed at the main entrance, and no one was admitted without permission.

At first I had to show my identification to enter, but they soon learned who I was and let me pass.

This building also had a frightening feature. Although it had a number of doors throughout, all except the main door were chained shut and padlocked. Even though it was a three-story building, there was only one door available for entrance and exit.

During the first week of school, students invited us to attend a back-to-school night performance, held in the basement of this building. There were no seats, so everyone had to stand. It was extremely crowded, with people so tightly packed into the small auditorium that we could scarcely move. Nevertheless, the students proudly escorting us managed to push us close to the front, the farthest from the door, the stairs, and the exit!

This was the first, and perhaps the only, frightening experience we had in China. Many Chinese love to smoke, and with the little freedom they have gained for themselves, they often smoke anywhere they please. Our fear was that someone who was smoking would start a fire in that crowded basement and we would all be trampled in the panic of trying to exit up the narrow stairs and out the one open door. It didn't happen, of course, and it was a good lesson for us, reminding us that God had brought us here, and He would care for us. He would not allow us to "dash [our] foot against a stone" (Psalm 9:12 KJV).

We never had trouble with our students attempting to smoke in class, and I was seldom afraid there again. I trusted God. But always in the back of my mind when I was teaching in that building was the thought that there was only one way out. I knew then, as I know now, He was the Way!

There was one practice that was more difficult for us to control in the classroom. The prevalence of dust and pollution cause many of the people to suffer from sinusitis and colds, particularly during the winter months. It is not unusual for them to cough, clear their throats, and spit on the ground or even the floor. It was disgusting to us. The more demure students spit into any wastepaper at hand. Very few could afford tissues. One student, sitting on the front row of my class, spit grandly on the floor in front of me. I was shocked, and reacted instantly.

"Don't you ever do that again in my classroom!" I blurted out. All the students froze. Usually well behaved in class, they were unaccustomed to their teachers chastising them, especially the American ones. They looked at me in disbelief. It was the only time I ever scolded a student, but the spitting never happened in my classroom again.

Few of our classroom experiences, however, were negative. Most were pleasant, some were humorous, and a few were glorious.

From the very first day of classes, Loren and I began a practice we never failed to follow. Each day before leaving the apartment, we prayed for each other. We asked that the Lord would be glorified in every thing we said and did, that the love of God would shine through us, and that our students would see Jesus in us.

At first we had no choice in what we taught. The Chinese government furnished the literature books and these were the basis on which the national testing of all college students was done. While we had no choice about the textbooks, occasionally a light would break through and shine on what the authorities had permitted us to do. When that happened during the discussions of their literature assignment,

God would open a door for us to share from the Bible. One such instance occurred in my advanced English literature class when a reading mentioned a doubting Thomas and included a reference to Jesus and His disciples. It was an open door! And I was prepared.

With much prayer, I took a copy of the Bible from which I read the story of the Crucifixion and the Resurrection of Jesus. He was with us in China!

Loren had a similar experience with his English-speaking class. His lesson was on the conjunction of the planets, and it included a reference to the Star of Bethlehem and the journey of the Magi. The author's conclusion was that there was no simple "logical" explanation for that particular star, leaving scientists still baffled about it.

Here was Loren's open door. As a former science teacher, he understood the significance of the lesson and the confusion of the scientists. From the Bible, he was able to read the story of the birth of Christ, giving much credence to the history of the Chinese in their knowledge of the skies and their study of astronomy. It was the Chinese, we believed, who had seen the Star as they observed the heavens and had followed it to Bethlehem.

I was having difficulty relating to the 107 students in my advanced English class. The university's administration wanted to get as many students into our classes as possible and had combined three classes into one. The students slept, talked, or did other lessons while I tried to lecture without a sound system. The lighting was poor. They couldn't see. They couldn't hear. The class was simply too big, and I had lost them.

Knowing how much the Chinese love to be entertained by foreigners, I decided to take my Autoharp to class and entertain my students. The lesson I brought to all my classes that day was on poetry. My lesson with the Autoharp was a last-ditch effort to hold the students' interest. In the end, it didn't work, and that particular class was split into the three sections, as it should have been from the beginning.

When I discovered my students' love of poetry, I projected Sara Teasdale's "The Falling Star" on a screen, using an overhead projector. It was a good oral exercise to have the students read aloud, since many of them were not very fluent in English yet. This I followed by singing and playing "Red River Valley." To my surprise, they knew and loved this song and eagerly sang along with me. Finally, I sang "In the Garden," changing the words from "the Son of God" to "the one I love." The words meant the same to me but had no religious significance to them and therefore would bring no offense. To them it was simply a beautiful love song. But He was in it! They were mesmerized. There was not a sound or a movement in the classes as I sang. God was opening the door to their hearts. We were bringing them His love. Difficult walls of prejudice and ancient tradition exist in China, and some of that hard ground had never broken. But barriers were beginning to fall, doors were beginning to open, and we were soon to walk right through.

11

Only Love and English Spoken Here

Following the arrival of our trunk came boxes of books and teaching materials we had shipped from home. In America we had grown accustomed to a wealth of teaching aids. No teacher expects to walk into a classroom devoid of materials. Not so in China.

"Bring your own resource materials," we were told. "Bring anything that can assist you in teaching students to speak and listen to English."

So we gathered materials.

Our postmaster shuddered to see us come. We had learned that books, magazines, and other printed materials could be shipped cheaply by Book Bag. This refers to the process of packing cartons and boxes of books and printed materials in large canvas bags for easy handling onboard ship. Although they had to travel by surface mail, they should arrive as soon as our trunk did, we were told. So we packed boxes as large as we could handle and made frequent trips to the post office.

We were aware that all mail could be censored, so we were careful not to include things the Chinese government might find offensive. We shipped large bundles of *National Geographic* and *Reader's Digest*, pictures, and maps. While much of these materials had been weeded and discarded from our schools' libraries at home, they would be invaluable in China.

Once we arrived, mail service was sporadic. Our letters often took two months to reach home, and mail sent to us was just as unpredictable. Copies of *Reader's Digest* and *Time* magazine, which we subscribed to for our own personal use, seldom arrived. Complaints to the Foreign Affairs Office fell on deaf ears. Somewhere along the postal route someone was enjoying our periodicals. The first year we were in China, we received only a few copies of these periodicals. Our boxes came, broken open but with their contents intact within the canvas bags.

Not all of our experiences with our students were problems, nor were they necessarily spiritual.

The day when the freshmen completed their military training and returned to campus was always a special one. Loren and I had started down to the market in Hai Shi Jiao when the long lines of young soldiers, both men and women, entered the gates of the campus. What a sight it was!

All young people in China are required to take some form of military training. Our students were really just children, mostly 17- and 18-year-olds. Some of them made a brave effort at looking adult. Others looked like they were playing dress-up in their fathers' uniforms.

The young men tried to look military. For the girls, it was another matter. They had not yet learned to march in a military style. Indeed, they "walked like girls!" Since all the uniforms were alike and made for males, they did little to flatter the girls. Perhaps to compensate, or perhaps from self-consciousness, they actually strutted as they walked with their military caps perched on the backs of their heads. We loved them from the start.

The upperclassmen were waiting for them too, greeting them with banners of welcome, music, and food during the specially declared Freshman Week. There were also parties and dances for the young cadets, which we did not attend. As far as we could discern, the new students experienced no hazing, as is customary on many US college and university campuses. Surely they had had enough of that kind of treatment by the teenaged gangs known as the Red Guards during the Cultural Revolution.

One of the most delightful experiences we had with our freshmen students was giving them names. All the Chinese young people seemed to want Western names. And not knowing Chinese, we realized that life would be much easier for us if we could identify each student by a name with which we were familiar. As Chinese names were foreign to us, they were difficult both to spell and to pronounce. So our first task with our new students was to give each a new name.

I'm not sure how Loren went about this, but I had a system. As each student told me his or her name, I would sound it out phonetically. Based upon the sound of the Chinese name, I would designate a Western name as close to it in sound as I could get. This system worked well with some of them, but not all. One of my dearest students was named Veronica. I never learned why. Perhaps someone else had given her the name. Or she may have chosen it for herself.

Some of the students preferred to choose their own names. Two stood out for their uniqueness. One in my class had chosen Iacocca because he desired to "make money and become rich." A young man in

Loren's class had chosen for himself the name of Hitler. I have read that our names influence our characters, and it was certainly true with Hitler. Sullen and rebellious, he seldom came to class, never turned in written work, nor appeared on testing day. Loren felt he had no alternative but to give him a failing grade.

Failing a university student is practically unheard of in China. Since all the students are chosen from the top 2 percent of secondary school graduates and are supported in college by the government, it is inconceivable that any should receive failing grades. All are passed, and all who do not drop out are graduated. This philosophy was a handicap to American teachers accustomed to evaluating their students. Without grades, students seemed to have little incentive to do their classwork or achieve success. The only incentive we saw was their desire to please us. And this the majority of them attempted to do.

Many of our lessons were great fun. Students in our speaking and listening classes loved to do skits, which were usually lively, funny, and made good use of the English usage lessons. One that I still laugh about was an exercise in which the students practiced ordering meals in an American restaurant. Among the resource materials we had brought from home were menus from American restaurants, including a popular national seafood chain.

Before Loren and I left the States, we had gone to this particular restaurant for a good-bye celebration. Their menus were very colorful, versatile, and tempting.

"How about taking some of these?" Loren suggested.

"Why?" I asked. "The students wouldn't be able to use them."

"That's the point," he explained. "We can show them how to order meals American-style. We can teach them how to calculate in American money and how to change yuan for dollars."

It was a good idea. When we approached the restaurant manager, he was excited too. He found a good supply of old menus to give us, which we jubilantly shipped off to China.

As the fall progressed and we had gotten into our routines, we remembered the menus.

The Chinese love to eat out. As we had learned, banqueting is a favorite pastime. When we approached our classes about the restaurant exercise using the menus, the students became excited.

We just had one problem. The Chinese serve all meals family-style, often eating from the main bowl with their chopsticks. The idea of ordering a meal just for oneself seemed selfish to them.

To make our lesson most successful, we decided to divide the class into groups of four or five and gave each student a monetary allowance and a menu. Each group was to select one student to serve as the waiter. Following the Cultural Revolution, many Chinese had come to feel that serving others was beneath their dignity so most of our students were reluctant to volunteer until they learned about tipping.

Ordinarily a group of four Chinese will order several main dishes consisting of pork, fish, and fowl, and share the dishes. As our diners began to make selections that appealed to them, and not understanding that side dishes normally come with an American meal, their totals began to skyrocket. One group had gone too far.

"How are you going to pay for all of this?" Loren asked them. "In America, if you can't pay, you might have to wash dishes," he laughingly informed them.

"Not me!" declared one bright boy. "You're my friend. I'll just borrow the money from you."

We informed them that the proper tip for a meal was 15 percent of the total on the check. One of my waiters who was obviously good at math figured out how much his 15 percent would be and began to manipulate his guests, allowing them to spend only 85 percent of their allowance. Iacocca's group ordered only appetizers and spent the rest of their money on drinks.

Since these were speaking and listening classes in English, it was against the rules to speak Chinese. But one student, corrected after lapsing back into Chinese several times, replied defensively that he had found a Chinese American restaurant in America and his waiter could only speak Chinese. Very creative, but it did not work. The teachers demanded English!

A great way to break the cultural barrier, this lesson also emphasized our motto, Only love and English spoken here!

Another skit I will never forget was done as a roast of the teacher.

I had developed what must have been either an irritating or an amusing habit of beginning every oral exercise by saying, "OK, here we go." I also had a habit of removing my glasses frequently. They bother me and I have never liked them. When I am able to be without them, even for a few minutes, I remove them. In class, I would often hold them in my hand as I taught. Eventually I came to see how ridiculous these two habits looked to my students.

Four of my brightest students were scheduled to give a skit in class. Three of them waited in the hall as Shirley, the leader, entered and approached me sheepishly.

"Mrs. Notley," she said hesitantly, "I hope you won't be offended by our skit."

Why would I possibly be upset? I wondered. Never had my students been rude or disrespectful.

"Would you mind taking a seat in the middle of the room?" she asked politely.

Ordinarily, I liked to sit on the front row for these skits in order to give them my full attention and evaluate them properly. It was not much to ask, I decided, so I moved back to the center of the room. As Shirley started out to join the other girls in the hall, she turned back abruptly.

"Oh, I forgot," she said. "May I use your notebook?"

I handed her the notebook.

"And your pen?"

I handed her the pen.

I was starting to get settled, but Shirley had not moved away.

"Well," I asked expectantly, "is that all?"

"Not quite. Your glasses."

Having stripped me of these important items, she walked away.

Instead of joining the other girls in the hall, Shirley stepped up to my desk, put on my glasses, and seated herself in my chair. I sensed that something interesting was about to happen.

The door opened and Evelyn and Donna entered.

"Good morning, girls," said Shirley pleasantly.

"Ni hao," the girls replied in Chinese, which was definitely against the rules.

"Excuse me?" Shirley responded curtly, eyes snapping as she removed the glasses.

"Sorry," they murmured sheepishly. "Good morning, Teacher."

"Please take your seats," she said, using the glasses to point to three chairs arranged before her.

She popped the glasses back on her nose.

Some of the students began to giggle and glance furtively at me. They knew whom she was imitating. So did I, though I tried not to laugh.

"Where's Virginia today?"

"She's sick."

The girls looked at each other with such guilty looks that I knew they were supposed to be lying for their friend.

Off came the glasses again.

"She always says she's sick. I doubt that she is," Shirley sighed, shaking her head. "She just likes to sleep late." I had noticed that my Chinese students often used illness as an excuse for sleeping late.

Back the glasses went on her nose.

The giggles grew louder.

Shirley looked up just as Virginia slipped into the room.

"Oh, there you are, Virginia. You're late!" she said, whipping off the glasses again.

"Let's get started." The glasses went back on the nose.

"Here we go!" she said with a whoop.

It was too much. The class began to howl. It had been a perfect parody of me. Any self-restraint the class had used was gone. We lost all control. It had been a joke on the American teacher.

Of course I laughed with them. But my heart sang. They loved me enough to laugh at me and know that I would laugh too. It was a victorious day for me.

The door had swung wide open.

12

The Buddhist Bell

Although fall was in the air, the weather was still warm when we went north to Anshan. It was China's National Day, and Foreign Affairs officials were taking us on our first sight-seeing trip to the central part of Liaoning Province. Anshan had been the headquarters of Norman Bethune, the Canadian doctor who brought modern medicine to China before the Cultural Revolution. The Chinese people honor him and have built a statue in his memory.

In Anshan we went mountain climbing on Qian-lian Shan (Thousand Lotus Hill). A most interesting and scenic place, in the midst of very flat land, a cone-shaped hill rises several hundred feet up into the air. Because Qianlian Shan is a great tourist attraction, we could not understand why, on their national holiday, we saw so few people attempting to climb it. The paths up the mountainside were steep and seemed little used. The higher we climbed, the more difficult they were to find and follow. We could ascend only by pulling ourselves up by grabbing onto small trees and shrubs. Eventually, we resorted to using tree roots and even rocks as handholds.

The people with us became concerned that I could not climb the mountain. Knowing my age, they wanted to lead me everywhere, holding onto me and helping me when I neither needed it nor wanted it. They didn't understand that I had grown up in the mountains of southeastern Oklahoma and had spent many joyous afternoons racing up the sides of the hills, following the faint paths which I fancied were known only to the wild things living there, and me. Loren used to tell others jokingly that when he married me I had one leg shorter than the other. When people looked sad and sympathetic, he would laugh and say it came from climbing up the sides of the mountains. I sometimes thought I must be part mountain goat because of my agility and my ability to climb up the sides of hills. I still could.

But to the Chinese, I was just an old woman who must be lifted up the mountain. At first, two of our friends would take hold of my arms, one on each side, depriving me of any ability I might have for balance. Because of this, my hands were not free to take hold of limbs to help pull myself up. Finally, I managed to shake them off, persuading them to let me do my own climbing.

Eventually we reached the top of the mountain where we found paved walks and terraces lined with rails and banisters leading to the top platform. The panoramic view was lovely. Although the day was not cloudless, the sky was an unbelievable blue festooned with fluff that scudded across it, which only enhanced its beauty.

Having gained the summit, we rested on the Immortals' Terrace as we listened to the Chinese fable associated with this mountain.

As the fable goes, two Immortals, the title Chinese give to their gods, had flown to the mountain on the backs of cranes. It was so beautiful that they decided to stay awhile and play a game of chess. We found that very profound!

What we had thought was a deserted mountain we saw to be crowded with throngs of people out to celebrate National Day. They had climbed the mountain too, but not with us. When we reached the summit, we found substantial stone steps carved into the opposite side of the mountain. The sensible Chinese had enjoyed a very comfortable climb.

Our sighs of relief at seeing a graceful way of descent were short-lived. We came up the back way. We would return the same way! So slowly and painstakingly, we descended by the same torturous route, holding onto the trees as we had in the ascent. We never did discover why our guides insisted on this backward climb. In the end, it didn't matter. When it was all over, we found that it was such a grand experience that we wouldn't have traded it for the easier climb. That was for those who were not out for an adventure. Our climb didn't hurt us and we had a day we would never forget.

But the day wasn't over yet. Once back on level ground, our escorts took us to visit a tenth-century Buddhist hermitage. Though Chairman Mao had tried to wipe out all practice of religion in China, the need to worship someone greater than oneself is deep-seated in the human spirit. Our search for God is as endless as time. And the Chinese people clung to their Buddhist faith.

The monastery had several buildings, small but lovely, built in the ancient Chinese style with tiled, horned roofs and bright colors. The horns on the roofs, we learned, were there to snag any demons who might try to slip down the roof and enter the sanctuary of the temple. Monks stood at the doors with candles and incense to sell to worshipers. We bought none, of course; but being brought up in church where the offering plate was essentially a part of every service, we dutifully dropped a few coins into their baskets.

In the courtyard stood a large, inverted stone bell with handles on each side. With an ear pressed against one handle, one could hear a most beautiful melody when gentle blows were struck against the opposite side. We were reminded of the Scripture that says that even the rocks will cry out in praise to Him Who made them.

It was all lovely except for the dark feeling we got when we looked at the old monks. They were so sad. Although they may have believed in some sort of paradise beyond death, their brooding faces belied any genuine faith in their gods. We discovered that one small room was reserved as a sort of death house where the very aged monks go to die. It was occupied that day, and we longed to tell the poor man inside of the hope of eternal life we have. As we walked from there into the bright sunlight of the beautiful flower garden, the words came to our minds, "The people living in darkness have seen a great light" (Matt. 4:16 NIV). Our hearts ached to tell them of that Light.

The strenuous climb on the backside of the mountain had left us stiff and sore, but Anshan was just the place to find relief. Although famous as the site of a great steel mill we also visited, far better for us was the fact that it was famous for therapeutic hot springs. Our escorts then took us to the Tanggangzi Hot Springs Resort where we were pampered and soaked in the hot mineral water baths. What a luxury! Relaxed and sleepy, we dozed happily in our soft-seat coach on the way back home, reveling in memories of our first real sight of China.

13

Coke and Christian Conversation

We soon realized that our desire to witness to the monks at Qianlian Shan was misdirected. Our call was to minister to the students in Dalian.

We had come to know some of our students, but the close personal relationship they had with other teachers had not opened itself up to us. We became a little discouraged. So we endeavored to get to know our students better.

Always the organized teachers, we made schedules for evening visits with the students in our home. Taking the calendar, we blocked off each evening into 30-minute sections. Then we allowed groups of three or four students at a time to schedule time with us to get acquainted, visit, and practice their English.

Each day when Loren and I returned from class, we would write in the names of the students who had requested time with us. There was one problem with this. Since we taught separate classes and had different sets of students, we often double scheduled. There were times when one or the other would fail to post the scheduled visitors on the calendar and then two sets of students would arrive at the same appointment time. Nevertheless, this method of having time with the students outside of class proved to be a great blessing.

At first we shared accounts of our families, theirs and ours, and stories about home. These students were not children of the one-child generation, though they would be forced to follow this regulation when they married. Occasionally they espoused a little sadness that their children would have no siblings and few cousins. To them, family was very important and, like people everywhere, they loved to talk about family gatherings during Chinese holidays.

Fall had finally come to Dalian, and the weather was disagreeable. Since there was little indoor heat in any of the buildings, we learned to layer our clothes. But this was not practical to do in our home. While we removed our coats when we reached home, our visitors preferred to keep theirs on.

Our apartment had hot water radiators for heating; but since we were on the top floor and hot water was often in short supply, the radiators were seldom warm. We had one solution. We had been given a two-burner gas hot plate for cooking. Knowing that humidity in the air makes a room more comfortable, we kept water boiling throughout the evening. On the rare occasions that the building had hot water, we would also fill the bathtub with water, which further added to the humidity and helped raise the temperature. Our Chinese visitors sometimes felt uncomfortably warm until we persuaded them to remove their coats.

Having them in our home became very important to our ministry. It was here that the Lord began to work in their hearts. It was another instance of the use of a gift He had given to us, the gift of hospitality.

A number of years before, Loren and I discovered that we had servant hearts and that God had given us the spiritual gift of hospitality. At times I had resented the fact that large groups of guests required large amounts of cooking, which I did primarily alone while others enjoyed the visits. But learning that this was a gift from the Lord changed my perspective completely. Then I understood why our home had always had an open door.

This was especially true concerning students from our local university. Our son, who was a student there, often brought his friends to our home. Sometimes they were just students who needed a safe haven, a place to go. They often frequented our house in the evenings, coming for holidays when they could not go home. Sometimes they were just looking for a home when homesickness became unbearable. For a number of years, while we worked on our lake house in the summer, we turned our home in town over to the college students. There they could live while they worked to make money for the coming year. We were used to having college students in our home.

And we were used to feeding them. Loren had a favorite saying, "Come to see us. We'll treat you so many ways, you'll have to like some of them." He usually meant, "Thelma's a good cook and there is plenty of food here." So we were accustomed to a house full of hungry students. Our Chinese students were just the latest.

Naturally, when these students came, we fed them. We praised the Lord for the popcorn cooker and a generous supply of popcorn. When we ran out of popcorn, we were able to purchase more at one of the movie theaters downtown. As with the widow's flour barrel and cruse of oil, we never ran out of popcorn. We had also found where we could purchase Coca-Cola. Chinese soft drinks seemed very diluted to us, and we preferred the stronger American drink. So did our students, although they could not afford them. We regularly purchased Cokes and served them to our students along with the popcorn.

Americans think they must have ice, even in winter, but our small refrigerator furnished us with only a limited amount. We learned quickly that our usual way of serving guests was not suitable for our Chinese students. They insisted on sharing the Coke, one can between two students. And no ice! To them, that was diluting the precious drink. Although they would take only one small glass of Coke apiece, they were welcome to all the popcorn they could eat. We began to fatten them up as we began to open their minds and God began to open their hearts.

When the students began to gather at the guesthouse for visits to our apartment at night, they were required to go through a ritual familiar to them but foreign to us. They had to sign in and out. Seated at a small table in the hotel lobby was the Communist Party chief. Students were required to surrender their identification cards to him, and he kept a record of who visited us and for how long. To us, this seemed an intrusion of privacy and we resented it at first. Little did we understand that the Lord had a hand in this as He did in all our activities. We later came to realize that problems caused by other foreign teachers were the cause of this scrutiny. In days to come, our treatment of our students and our honesty with the university seemed to change this philosophy. We were there for a purpose. It was greater than we ever dreamed and it was never thwarted.

Small groups of students came to visit at first, then more and more students requested time. We were careful about the topics we discussed. But as the winter progressed, some of the students brought Bibles into our rooms and asked that we teach them. It was a joy to answer their simple questions. Especially dear were the girls from my speaking and listening class. I believed that they had tested me, and had I not responded openly and lovingly, they would have been afraid to approach us.

This was the beginning. This was what God had been preparing us for through all of those years of teaching in America. We finally understood what witnessing was all about. We were sharing Him and His Love with those who had never really heard of Him before. We were beginning to break new ground. By so doing, God's love within us was leaping to new heights.

It would be one of the greatest times of our lives.

14

China Thanksgiving

The snow fell soft on Changchun
The day we traveled there.
A dusting fine as sugar fell
Like frosting on our hair.

It came at dusk like eiderdown
And nestled in the trees.
It wrapped the town in an ermine gown
But couldn't our laughter freeze.

We walked the lane in glistening white.
Streetlights with halos glowed.
We sang of winter wonderlands
And sleighs our grandfathers rode.

The children sang of Grandma's house,
Hearts turned to homes so dear.
Then lifted up in praise to Him
Whose love had brought us here.

—Thelma Notley

Early in our stay in China we became aware of an energy shortage. Electricity was often undependable, and we grew accustomed to blackouts in the early evening. If we were attempting to read or grade papers, we would be temporarily defeated. So we began to rely heavily on candles. But we had not thought to bring candleholders with us.

Always the collector, Loren found four empty decorative wine bottles to use for this purpose. We laughed at what we imagined our Baptist mothers would say if they could see such bottles gracing our home. But we were thankful for them. When the electricity went off, we would light the four candles and break out the cards. We could see well enough to play cards by candlelight, but I didn't really enjoy the game at first because Loren beat me every time. As a minister's daughter, I was never allowed to play cards as a child, and it was not one of my better skills.

"Why don't you let me win sometimes?" I complained.

"It wouldn't be much fun if I just let you win," he laughed.

"Well, it's no fun losing all the time," I whined. "I thought we came to China to show love. What kind of love is this?" It was really hard to make him feel guilty, especially over a card game whose name was Spite and Malice.

"You are just being spiteful and full of malice!" I grumbled.

"It's the name of the game," he replied, laughing as he beat me again.

So, with *no* charity but plenty of "spite and malice" in his heart and very little enthusiasm in mine, we continued to play in the subdued light until the power came back on. I must confess that until I improved my cardplaying skills, I found the game boring.

Interestingly, we found that the candles were a testimony to our faith in God. All of our fellow Chinese teachers understood that we were Christian. Though they knew little or nothing about the Bible or our faith, they knew we practiced it and they respected us for it. One day one of our friends was visiting with us when she noticed the candles, burned to different levels and sitting in a group on Loren's desk.

"May I ask you something personal?" she asked.

"Of course! Ask away!" We wanted our lives to be an open book before our Chinese friends.

"What is the religious significance of your candles?" she asked.

"So we can see when the power goes off," Loren replied.

We all laughed, but inwardly we rejoiced that our friend perceived a spiritual atmosphere in our home and knew without being told that the Lord was there.

The unpredictability of electricity was a problem in every home. Since we had been supplied with a gas hot plate, the school could not understand why I also wanted an electric oven. I was used to baking at home; and with fall in the air and bananas and apples in the market, we longed for banana bread and apple pie. But in all of our shopping trips about town, we were never able to find a small electric toaster oven. They just weren't on the market. Much later we discovered that although they were not actually against the law, most Chinese frowned on them because of the energy they used. So none of the housewives used them. But I *wanted* one.

Having a network of friends about the province presents a distinct advantage. To our delight, when Rosanna went to another city to visit some of our China family, she returned bringing me an electric oven. What fun I had baking biscuits and banana bread! During one baking session, however, the power went off in our part of town and my banana bread was only half done. I left it in the oven until the power came back on and then finished baking it. It was OK, but did not rise like it should. It was still banana bread.

The lack of any kind of solid shortening presented still another problem. Everything tasted like the oil we had to use. Search as I might, I never found shortening on the market. One day while I was studying the problem, I remembered my mother's solution. Growing up in the country during the rationing days of World War II, many things were not available when I was a girl. But we raised our own meat and always had an ample supply of chicken, rabbits, milk, and cream. And pork! We raised pigs.

In the fall, neighbors would gather at slaughtering time. It was always an exciting day and we knew we would eat well that night. The resulting fresh meat was usually pork chops or pork roast, and we hung the ham and shoulders in the washhouse to cure. Dad loved Canadian bacon, and this expensive cut of meat was free to us. Mother ground the lean, scrappy parts to make a tasty sausage. We had no way of freezing the meat, so Mother cooked all the sausage and packed it into quart canning jars, covered it with the excess fat, and sealed it for winter. It kept beautifully. She must have learned this from her own mother on the wheat farm in western Oklahoma where she was raised. We dined richly. So much butter and fat never seemed to harm my parents, lifelong Christian servants. My father lived into his 80s, and Mother passed away at 98, eating as she had all her life.

When Loren and I shopped in a local store in Hai Shi Jiao, we usually passed by the meat counter because we refused to eat fresh meat. One day, though, I noticed mounds of white fat out on the butcher's counter, and a light dawned. Why couldn't I render up some lard as we had when I was a child? When we asked for five kilos of the fat, the butcher blinked. The Chinese considered fat a delicacy and used it very sparingly. Questioning me to see if I had not made a mistake, he measured the fat, which we carried home triumphantly. I rendered it and we had shortening at last! White and sweet, it never lasted long enough to get rancid. We used it to fry apples, potatoes, and eggs, and the baked goods we made with it in tasted like home.

The "cook" was finally in business!

Dalian is famous throughout the land as the Apple Basket of China, each fall producing an abundance of the tasty fruit. Apples seemed to be everywhere. We often bought small quantities at the market, but we were told that our Department of Foreign Affairs would provide us with a good winter's supply. And we believed it.

Operating true to form, however, our director told us he couldn't get us any. Of course we didn't believe him. He had supplied apples in the past and we knew he could get them for us if he chose. We couldn't persuade him. He just didn't choose! But there was one among us he seemed to respect, Rosanna! So, with a lot of cajoling, she persuaded him to find apples for us.

It was late in the season before our apples were delivered to us. Although they were very expensive by Chinese standards, they did not look very good. They were apples, nonetheless, and they tasted wonderful! There was just one problem with them. Packed in baskets with straw from a farmer's chicken yard, they carried an unbearable stench! After we removed the apples from the baskets and threw away the baskets and the straw, we spread the apples out on newspaper on the floor to air while we went to Changchun for Thanksgiving. Eventually we wrapped each one in newspaper, as we do with pears at home, and packed them down in cleaner baskets so that they lasted through the winter.

Because Thanksgiving is strictly an American holiday, the Chinese do not observe it. We did, however, receive a long weekend off so that we could celebrate it with our China family. We had been invited to gather in Changchun for the familiar feast.

Anything American fascinated our students, and we had received permission from the school to talk with them about those things that make American life unique. Thanksgiving, of course, was one of them. So the doors opened for us to share with them the history and meaning of the American Thanksgiving. Although this national holiday has lost something of its original religious significance in America, we were excited about explaining to our students the true meaning of the day, that of giving thanks to God for His blessings to us.

Not only did we receive permission to teach about Thanksgiving, we were encouraged to do so, opening future doors of opportunity. This caused no offense and resulted in other invitations to speak of our life in America in the months to come. Since our students loved to sing, we took this opportunity to teach them some Thanksgiving songs. Using pictures and stories about the first Thanksgiving, our students also learned about the Pilgrims and Native American Indians.

Our trip to Changchun for Thanksgiving was a great deal of fun. Loren and I had not yet attempted to purchase train tickets and did not know how to go about it. How thankful we were for Rosanna, who knew just how. It involved standing in lines at the depot ticket window for long periods of time and often doing verbal battle with the ticket seller. But Rosanna was persistent, and we soon were on our way.

We took a soft sleeper on Wednesday evening and arrived in Changchun the next morning. We awoke to a lovely surprise. It was snowing! The ground was white with the gentle shower that lasted throughout the entire weekend, sometimes falling like fine powder and at other times coming down in large, fluffy flakes like goose down. Unlike Dalian, there was no wind to chill us and we gloried in the beauty of our first sight of snow in China. It seemed a gift from our Father.

While it was lovely in the daytime, the softly falling snow wrapping the city in a hush, it was even more beautiful at night as we walked down the quiet streets under streetlamps with halos of falling snow. We bundled ourselves from head to toe with only our noses showing. Like children, we walked in the snow laughing and singing "Winter Wonderland"; "Let It Snow"; and, of course, "Silent Night."

It was enchanting!

By Saturday our entire "family," 61 in all, had arrived. Single teachers, couples, and families with children ranging in ages from 1 to 10 joined together for this celebration. The children were as happy to see each other as we adults were. Most of them lived where there were no other American or English-speaking children, so they joyfully laughed and played in the snow. They built snow forts. They threw snowballs. They had battles.

Once when I was crossing their battleground, they wanted to know which side I was on. Luckily I was able to dart into a doorway before they could attack me. They were all beautiful and delightful, and made us think of our own children at home. One family with three precious little girls had asked us to bring peanut butter and laundry detergent from Dalian. They could not get these things where they lived. As a treat for these little ones, I brought banana pudding from our "magic trunk" supply, to which I added fresh bananas. It was a treat they had not enjoyed since leaving America. They loved me for it, and all the rest of the evening there were hugs for "Grandma Notley."

On Saturday we spread our feast. While there was no turkey, we had plenty of chicken, duck, dressing, candied sweet potatoes, mashed potatoes, gravy, salads, and desserts. It was a typical American Thanksgiving dinner. Loren's and my contribution included our old standby, brown beans and ham. No one could believe that the Notleys had pinto beans since they were very hard to find in China. Along with all the other good food, they were soon devoured. Though there were no pumpkins in China then, we also took sweet potato pie, a big hit. No one could tell it wasn't pumpkin. No one cared. The women wanted to know what made the crust so tender and flaky, so happily I passed on Mother's lesson in rendering lard.

It was a wonderful time of fellowship, with hymns and stories and entertainment by the children, who sang Thanksgiving songs. One bright youngster recited a lengthy poem in perfect Chinese. Finally came the breaking of a turkey piñata, followed by a wild scramble for the candy. We felt almost like we were at home.

The final joy of our Thanksgiving trip was waiting for us when we returned home to Dalian. Because a coal furnace had heated our hotel room in

Changchun, the room was smoky and had a distinct odor, which we and our clothes absorbed. To our distress, when we returned to Dalian, we had no water. As a matter of fact, there had been none for three days.

We had learned to conserve water early on. By filling the bathtub, we always had water to use for washing hands, faces, and dishes, and even for flushing the toilet. We had also learned to pour the excess consumable water from the thermoses into pitchers and water bottles. But until the water came back on, we were reduced to "rotating" our clothing and standing back from one another!

Often in the days since, as I slowly baste the turkey at home or pull pumpkin pies from the oven, I think back to that wonderful day.

It was a Thanksgiving day like no other.

He was there.

15

Making Disciples

Winter had come to Dalian, prompting us to dress for cold weather and try to keep warm any way we could. Since it was not very warm in the apartment, we made good use of the heavy fleece warm-ups and sometimes even wore our jackets inside.

When we returned from our Thanksgiving celebration in Changchun, we realized it was time to push our beds together and hooked up the electric blanket. As the nights grew colder, we snuggled down in its warmth. Soon, however, the air in our apartment was so frigid that we were forced to take our work to bed, propping up with pillows so we could read or grade papers in its lovely warmth. Frequently Loren would give credit where credit was due.

"Honey," he would purr, "I'm so glad you insisted on bringing this blanket!"

Even though our bodies thawed out in our fleece suits warmed by the blanket, we needed our hands above cover. That didn't seem to bother Loren, but I found my hands becoming stiff with the cold. What was I to do when I could not hold up the book I was reading? The solution was simple: gloves! The gloves we had brought with us, however, were heavy woolen ones, bulky and cumbersome, making it difficult to hold a pencil to grade papers or to turn the pages of a book.

One day, observing the wonderful women who swept the streets and sidewalks to keep the campus and the city clean, I saw my answer—the working women's white cotton gloves! Not only were they light, they made movement easy; and they were available at the campus store. At last, I was in business.

Our classrooms were usually cold too, sometimes even frigid, producing a chilling effect not only on our bodies but also on our spirits. Thanksgiving had taken us on a high, and we were coming down. But God knew where we were, and He had things for us to do. Besides our heavy teaching loads, we were asked to do things we felt were above and beyond the call of duty.

In addition to my student classes, I was asked to work with a group of young English teachers who did not understand their lessons. Many of the words were difficult for them, and often the meanings were vague. I was turning into an interpreter. At first we met in one of the empty classrooms; but as the weather cooled, I invited them to come to our apartment where it was warmer. It would be less formal, I reasoned. I would serve them tea and get to know them.

They were lovely women and the plan worked well. One of them had immigrated from Korea where Christianity was on the rise. As the fall progressed, they became less inhibited and began to ask me about the Bible.

Besides this class, the Foreign Language Department asked us to take on other extracurricular activities. And Loren was asked to tape and interpret Voice of America and British Broadcasting Company programs for one of the professors. Regardless of any explanation Loren might give for the words and phrases, the professor insisted on arguing with him.

We wondered, since he already seemed to have the interpretations fixed in his mind, why he bothered to come to Loren at all.

Eventually the man gave up and left Loren alone. We decided that he thought Loren knew little about the topics being broadcast. It was just as well. His mind was already made up before he came. Loren would never have been able to explain things to him against his will. It was just another example of the Chinese mind. We simply didn't understand it.

As we moved into the winter and encouraged our students to visit us at night, we began to see not just our first- and second-year students but also some who were older. A few were not even in our classes, but they desired to be with us. They said they wanted to practice their English, but we felt they were hungry for something else, something they sensed we could give them.

Christmas approached. Our apartment must have carried something of a holiday atmosphere, for more and more students came to see us. One young man, who did not fit the regular role of the other students, began to cultivate our acquaintance.

Jack was the son of a professor of ancient history in another university. Just hearing about it made my mouth water. The professor came with Jack once to visit us and I longed to sit at his feet as he told of the ancient dynasties. Wicked at times, they nonetheless held an air of romance our Western histories lack. But Jack was not interested in history. He was looking for something far older and more lasting.

My first impression of him was that he really didn't look very Chinese. He was tall and a little awkward. As with most of the young people, he was very thin. He even looked somewhat austere. And he played a trick on us.

"Are you interested in Chinese art?" he asked.

Of course, I was interested in everything Chinese.

"Would you like to meet an artist friend of mine and see some of his paintings?"

What a foolish question! We bit immediately.

At an appointed time, he took us by bus to a nondescript apartment in an unfamiliar part of town. If not naive, at least we were trusting souls. We had put ourselves completely in his hands.

The artist's studio was not what I had expected. I had imagined a typical Western studio. Of course it was not Western! We were in China. The rooms were faintly lit, as were most homes in China due to the scarcity of energy and the need to conserve power.

What the artist showed us was not what we had expected. I'm not sure what we expected, but not the long scrolls of stylized art I now recognize as classical Chinese. He showed us scrolls of flowers and birds and animals, primarily horses. Though they were not particularly to our liking, we pretended to admire them. Then came the punch line. Our young man had brought us there to buy.

Embarrassed and a little angry, we felt compelled to select some of the scrolls. After all, we were "rich Americans" and could hardly refuse the sales pitch. We selected scrolls with large pink camellias on them and fled. We had been fleeced!

Later, we came to see God's plan in it all.

Our young merchant came to visit us again and again. We had neither disappointed nor dishonored him before his artist friend. He had kept his word to his friend—we had bought his paintings. Not only had we bought them, we had hung them in a very prominent place in our living room. We had honored the young man. As our relationship grew, so did his understanding of the source of our love and concern for him. Together we would genuinely celebrate the true Gift of Christmas that year.

God had still other work for us to do, this time through private tutoring. The dean of the Foreign Language Department, who had become our friend, asked me to tutor the daughter of the president of a university in another city. A sweet girl, she was having a lot of trouble with English. I worked with her for quite some time and never felt we made any headway, although both her father and our friend felt that the time spent was worthwhile. I would not allow her to pay me because the work was in line with my teaching duties. But she gave me several lovely gifts I never felt I deserved. She came only one semester and I never saw her again.

Loren had better luck. President Li had "taken a likin'" to him. Often they met in the garden between our building and his. I suppose he enjoyed practicing his English with Loren.

Loren was collecting again. He "collected" President Li!

President Li asked Loren to tutor one of his students and he gladly agreed. The young man was a special protégé of the president who had been tutoring him privately. Soon to receive his master's degree, he was already a published author. A delightful young man with a brilliant mind, he seemed already to have accomplished what we supposed he had come for. There was little we could teach him about the English language. He wanted to move on to better things. He wanted to talk to us about the Bible.

We were on shaky ground.

But our God is faithful. We had come at His command. Our boldness had never trapped us. Our trust in Him was all the protection we had. So, praying

Peter's prayer of boldness, we waded right in. We opened the Bible to him.

As if by the Lord's design, the young man's name was Paul. Delighted, we read to him the beautiful story of Saul of Tarsus whose name the Lord had changed to Paul and who had become the greatest missionary the world has ever known. We gave him a Bible, one of many we eventually gave away.

At first we felt he was slow to receive what he read. Later, we realized that this was a result of his brilliant intellect. As he read, he examined every word in minute detail, dissecting every phrase. To us this was tedious, but this scrutiny was his way of studying English.

What a joy Paul was! The evenings spent with him not only opened his understanding but ours as well. His great desire seemed to be to discern and absorb perfectly every word of the Scriptures.

"The Bible is the greatest book I have ever read," he declared excitedly one evening. Paul became hungry for the Word. "Maybe God will use *me* to take the story of Jesus all over China!" he exclaimed.

Knowing the danger of open testimony, especially that of prominent people, we were amazed at his excitement and eagerness to share the "forbidden" story of Jesus and His great love.

Paul finished his degree soon afterward and we never saw him again. But I know that someday we shall meet again, and he will have wonderful stories to tell of how God used him to spread the gospel throughout this beloved land.

16

Christmas

This is My Father's world, the whole of it.
A sacred honor gave He to these men,
For from the East He called those ancient ones
To worship at His crib in Bethlehem.
—Thelma Notley

Christmas promised to be a time we would know whether we had weathered our culture shock and our separation from home and family. We would know with certainty if we were where we were really supposed to be.

No carols played in the department stores or over the radio, no Christmas lights shone on street corners or from the windows of homes. Would it seem like Christmas without these outward signs of the holidays? Had we become so accustomed to the commercial aspects of the season that without them it would have lost its lovely aura? It would be a time of testing for us.

One thing hadn't changed. It was the birthday of Jesus no matter where we were. But God knew that in our humanity we still needed some symbols, and He provided them. As Loren walked through the classroom building one morning, something caught his eye through the open door to the Drama Department. Of course, he had to investigate! What he saw were stage props, among them a small artificial evergreen tree set in a tub of plaster of paris. It was the answer to the silent yearnings of our hearts.

It was a Christmas tree!

Federal law protects all trees in China, and cutting any kind of tree is a federal offense. So, live Christmas trees for westerners are prohibited. We knew teachers whose students, in the dark of night, brought them small evergreens. But not us. We discouraged it. We would break no laws or be a party to any such thing. The commandments were binding in China too.

Promising to return the artificial tree to the Drama Department after Christmas, Loren proudly carried it home and set it in a place of honor on his desk. It became a magnet, the instrument through which we could share the story of Jesus' birth with visitors to our home.

But what were we to do for decorations?

Although the department stores downtown had strings of colored lights, they refused to sell them to us. At first we didn't understand why, but eventually we discovered that they were reserving them for their own use, as the Chinese decorate lavishly for their greatest holiday, Chinese New Year. Fortunately, my propensity to plan ahead again paid off. Included in the "magic trunk" were a string of minilights, some hard candies, and several packages of gum. Thanks to Loren's resourcefulness with the extension cords he had made, we strung the lights on the tree, and with bows of crinkled ribbon we hung the colored candies and bright packages of gum as ornaments. Christmas cards, which had begun to arrive from home and from our students, stood among the branches. The tub of plaster of paris was unsightly, so we wrapped Loren's red flannel shirt around it like a tree skirt.

We had our Christmas tree! Christmas was turning out to be wonderful!

Although the tree was definitely a drawing card, it was not the only attraction. As the influx of Christmas cards grew greater, we began to tape them to the walls. And as a doorway to our vast new adopted country, I had hung above my desk a large map of China. Through it we were able to understand where we were in proximity to others of our group. Above the map we placed a card depicting a glorious Herald Angel so that he seemed to be covering China with the good news of the birth of the Savior.

A Christmas tree is not really complete without packages beneath it. Soon we had those too. Our daughter Laura had shipped us an ample supply of oatmeal, and included in the package was Loren's favorite candy, licorice sticks. Fellow teachers Joe, Joan, and Brenda also sent gifts, a safari hat for Loren and an embroidery thread box and sweatshirt for me, which would later open the door to an interesting conversation.

Beneath the tree were even better things than the brightly wrapped packages, including a small Nativity scene. As our guests looked at the tiny figures, they wanted to know the significance of each one. It was then that we were able to tell the story of Christmas in all its glory.

We felt the depth and the beauty of the Redemption story fully with the most moving card we received from home. It came from Alma, a fellow teacher who had also served in China, and contained the ultimate Christmas story, John 3:16.

"For God *(the greatest person)* so loved *(the greatest degree)* the world *(the greatest company)*, that he gave *(the greatest act)* his only begotten Son *(the greatest gift)*, that whosoever *(the greatest opportunity)* believeth *(the greatest simplicity)* in him *(the greatest attraction)* should not perish *(the greatest promise)*, but *(the greatest difference)* have *(the greatest certainty)* everlasting life *(the greatest possession)*."

This card we placed under the tree and near the manger scene. As students picked it up, they read it in awe. A Christmas blessing we received from Jack reflected this same message. When we told our students of God's great love for China, they looked at us with wonder. Love, to them, was supposed to be bad, to be selfish. This was the most unselfish act of love they had ever heard of. One thing that seemed to impress them was that the wise men were called from "the east."

"We like to think that God called men from China to be present at the birth of His Son," we suggested as tears formed in their eyes. They could accept the story of the Wise Men because the ancient Chinese scholars were known to be great astrologers and believed in the prophetic powers of the stars. Our students were amazed to hear that such a great honor may have been given to the Chinese by God at Christ's birth. They began to understand the depth of the love God has for China.

"China needs a celebration like this," they said.

We knew it!

Christmas opened the door to what would become the greatest work we had ever done. In the days to come, Satan tried to move us on. But God would not let us go. He was not yet finished with us in China.

Christmas in China was indeed wonderful, and we were never homesick.

17

China Call

There must have been a part of me
That fell in love with the sea
When I was but a tiny child,
The pull is so strong on me.

I cannot see the breakers crash
Or hear the seagull crying
Without they call me, "Come away
To where the fish are flying!

"To lands where golden dreams await,
To islands wrapped in blue,
Where ginger blossoms big as plates
Drip honey down with dew!"

I sailed at last the laughing sea
Across the world of blue.
I came at last to Old Cathay,
My childhood dream come true.

—Thelma Notley

He listened to my "changing money" conversation with the bank teller. He set up his work station in the warm lobby of the guesthouse and watched us come and go. He relieved the students of their identification cards when they came to us night after night. He kept a record of everyone who visited us.

He watched us carefully. We were both suspicious and a little fearful of him. He had power and we knew it.

He was the local Communist Party chief.

We never dreamed he would use his power to aid us.

School was out for the Chinese New Year holiday. The students, like college students everywhere, had fled the campus for the long winter holiday at home. We were left alone, but not for long. Soon, some of our fellow American teachers began to arrive. We had great plans to travel together to "see China." One friend was the son of former missionaries and had grown up in China. He promised to act as guide as we traveled down the southeast coast, visiting some of the wonderful places we had read about. We could hardly wait!

Our holiday began as planned. We would go by sea down to Shanghai. After a few days of sight-seeing in Shanghai, we would board the Iron Rooster and travel by rail down to Guangzhou (old Canton). Along the way we would visit our friend's childhood home. At Guangzhou we would cross over to Hong Kong for our winter conference and reunion with our entire group. At least, this was the plan. But it was never to happen.

The tickets for our boat trip to Shanghai had been purchased. We would leave from the port of Dalian, go through the Bo Hai Bay, out to the Yellow Sea, and down to the great port of Shanghai on the Huangpu (Yellow River). Our bags were packed and we had only to get to the port, board our ship, and be on our way. But we had a problem. We couldn't get transportation to the port.

It was a holiday. It was night. There were no minivans or drivers on duty on campus. The school personnel, like the students, were gone. No one was in charge. Furthermore, no taxis would come to the campus. We were stranded. The time for the ship to sail was rapidly approaching. We were in danger of missing the boat. It was then that we knew that the Lord had put the Communist Party official in our lives for a purpose.

He was sitting in the lobby as we dashed frantically about attempting to find transportation. Seeing our frustration at the refusal of the taxis to come to the campus, with quiet efficiency he made a phone call, and soon two taxis arrived at the door of the guesthouse. We quickly loaded and arrived at the port with time to spare. He had become another "angel" to us. He had been used to deliver us.

With great relief we boarded the ship, found our state rooms, and went to bed. We went to sleep sailing through the blue Bo Hai Bay and woke up on the turbulent Yellow Sea. Its name is well deserved, for it looked to us like a great sea of yellow mud. How anything could live in such polluted water was a mystery to us. It looked like the topsoil of all China was pouring down the Yellow River and emptying into the ocean.

A day and another night brought us into Shanghai. Although the ship berthed in the middle of the night, it was in the predawn hours that we gathered our belongings and made our way ashore. As is typical, there were no streetlights and we stumbled our way toward town. We had hotel reservations, but we could find no taxis at that hour. How were we to find our way? Eventually a small open cab stopped for us and took us to our hotel. We then learned that we must alter our plans. Our friends had to leave us to find medical help for one of the group. We would not be going together down the coast as planned. Loren and I would be alone.

Left on our own again, we were in a quandary about what to do. With prayer in our hearts and a China guidebook in our hands, we decided to "see China." Two old people who could not speak Chinese, we were adrift on that huge continent amongst over 1 billion people who could not speak English. It seemed that most of them were on the move for Spring Festival. Before our trip was over, we believed we had met most of them in the train stations trying to purchase tickets.

It is difficult for most Americans to appreciate the ease with which we travel in our country. But in China, whether traveling by ship, plane, or train, braving great mobs of people and standing in long lines to get tickets are commonplace. Our more experienced friends informed us that it was impossible to purchase tickets in less than three days. Often, they warned, people stood in long lines for hours only to learn after reaching the ticket window that all available space had been sold. We determined to stay in constant touch with the Lord, our "Travel Agent," Who often "parted the waters" and opened the way for us.

Having a great desire to visit western China, and with five weeks of freedom to go and do as we liked, we booked an air flight to Chengdu. It was the memorable beginning to carefree and fun-filled days. We were going to see China!

We landed several miles from the city after dark in this strange land, alone without interpreters at an airport devoid of lights. The little light we saw came from a fenced enclosure where our baggage had been deposited. Claiming our luggage, which was locked inside the fenced building, became our first problem and our first lesson in "acting on our own." We could do nothing but clasp hands, pray, and "agree" that the authorities would understand us and release our bags. Then Loren pushed his way through the crowd that always swarms around foreigners and somehow retrieved our bags. But we were miles out in the country. How were we to get to town?

Taxi drivers wanting 60 or 70 yuan ($30 to $40) to take us to town surrounded us. But some of the gracious people around us indicated that we should board one of the buses parked in the dark a block away.

I'm afraid my trust in the Lord began to waver just a bit. As the bus moved out into the countryside, we were not sure exactly where we were going. Wobbling my way to the front of the bus, I opened the guidebook to the city of Chengdu and pointed to the Jinjiang, the name of our hotel, hoping the driver would understand that was where we wished to go. Brusquely he waved me back to my seat. Loren just folded his arms, sat back, and trusted the driver. The longer we rode, the more unsure I became. Approaching the driver again, I tried to communicate our destination. Again he waved me back to my seat. When I approached him for the third time, he became angry with me so I sat down, resigned to accept whatever happened to us in this strange land. Eventually the lights of an elegant hotel came into view and the driver delivered us to the door of the Jinjiang Guesthouse, reminding me Who was in charge of our travel plans. Never again on this trip was I tempted to worry. God would bring us safely through.

Chengdu offered us the finest Chinese architecture we would see in China, via the West China Medical College. Constructed around the turn of the century as a mission school, it had remained miraculously untouched during the Cultural Revolution and was still in excellent condition. Its tiled horned roofs and its walls, doors, and windows painted in brilliant colors were beautiful. It was the first school we visited on our trip. And it was here that we first received contract offers to come and teach.

A short walk from our hotel we found a wonderful open-air market. The day was rainy and we seemed to wade in the mire as we passed through large flocks of all kinds of fowl, crying and preening and showing themselves off to prospective customers. Here we also found the usual meat market with the meat hung out, exposed to the elements, as well as huge mounds of beautiful fruits and vegetables. Most amusing was the display of hog heads and tails floating in a tank of water waiting to be sold. These "little piggies" really did "go to market."

The purchase of tickets to our next destination, Chongqing, promised to take three days. Instead, after earnest prayer, an "angel" came our way, the first we would meet on this trip. She got tickets on a soft sleeper for us for the evening of the third day, the exact time we wished to leave. In our minds we kept hearing the warning of the younger and more seasoned travelers who said, "It's impossible to get tickets within three days of your first attempt." Not so when you have the Lord as "Expert Travel Agent" working for you! We were comfortably tucked into our berths by bedtime.

By the next morning we were in Chongqing, called the Chinatown of China. Located in the confluence of the Jialing and Yangtze Rivers, it is very humid and is known as the Furnace of the Yangtze. Chongqing was unlike any of the other cities we visited, which boasted modern downtown business districts. Very little Western influence exists in Chongqing, with few contemporary conveniences or dress. Indeed, there seemed to be very little of this city that looked modern. With its narrow, winding streets and flights of steps, it was definitely China. The Nationalist seat of government during World War II, Chongqing had been the wartime capital of Chiang Kai-shek's Kuomintang government until 1945.

It was from Chongqing the "scouts" came to us in September from the Institute of Industry Management to entice us away from Dongbei. They tempted us with wonderful contracts and an apartment with an outside entrance where students could visit us without scrutiny. A large living room would be ideal for group meetings, and we would also have a modern kitchen with a large refrigerator. The school would pay for our transportation and ship all our household goods. Discussing the opportunity they offered us, we took the contracts with us, promising to let them know later.

"We cannot come this year," Loren told them. "We are under contracts to Dongbei. We will not break them. Perhaps next year."

"You can break the contracts," they told us. "All contracts are actually with the Department of Education in Beijing. It really doesn't matter where you teach. All contracts are the same."

"Sorry," we said. "Perhaps next year."

It was nice to be wanted.

Again God sent us an "angel" in the form of Chongqing's Foreign Affairs officer, who had no obligation to us but graciously helped us get tickets to Kunming when we were ready to leave. Again, we avoided the typical three-day wait.

We had not yet seen the most enticing city, which held for us the greatest temptation we would face. Kunming, known as Spring City, was beautiful.

Although it was January, the weather was warm and balmy, and flowers bloomed everywhere. The people in this area, many of whom are minorities who migrated from Burma, Laos, and Thailand, are happy and friendly people. It was a delight to be among them. Being of the World War II generation, Loren and I were able to identify with Kunming. It was on the Burma Road, and the base for the American Flying Tigers.

Kunming's women produce and sell beautiful crafts. Especially interesting are the handcrafted bags and aprons, and being a quilter and crafter myself, I succumbed with delight when I saw them. I became an easy target for these lovely women to approach on the street for a sale. If we had problems with the money, they were eager to "changee monee." In fact, everywhere we turned, industrious young women approached us with outstretched hands asking, "Changee monee?" One woman wanted to be my friend, which meant I must tell her my age. Revealing her age first as 53, she seemed surprised and a little doubtful when I told her I was 60.

Looking at these wonderful people dressed in their colorful, ethnic costumes convinced me: *I needed* a dress like that! Loren had great fun encouraging me and helping me to try one on, right in the aisle of the store. It is one of the purchases I treasure most. It resembles nothing in America. It is authentically Chinese.

What did seem American to me was the appearance of the people in this part of China. When I was in college, I had done a study exploring the possible origins of the Native American Indians. I believed then, and am more convinced now, that they migrated from the Far East. Everywhere we looked we seemed to see the faces of our friends at home.

Growing up with Native American Indians in Oklahoma, we never thought consciously about racial differences. They were just our friends; there was no prejudice with us as children. It was never taught in my home. Perhaps it was this resemblance to those we knew and loved at home that helped us feel so comfortable and at home in China.

Another interesting similarity between the Chinese and the early Native American Indians lies in the way they care for their small children. The split pant the Chinese use for their infants reminds us that primitive Native American Indian women did not use diapers either. And, just as the Native American Indian mothers carried their papooses, these young mothers also carry their babies on their backs. Halfway around the world, they do not seem so far apart.

Located near Kunming is China's Stone Forest, a fantastic formation of limestone thrust up into perpendicular structures many stories high by an ancient sea 270 million years ago. In this "forest" we found deep pools of water and many pavilions for rest stops. Tribesmen brought in camels for the tourists to be photographed on or for the more adventurous to ride. Very exotic, it was much different from what we had seen in the rest of China. There was even a Stone Forest "taxi," an open horse-drawn carriage reminiscent of *Oklahoma*'s "The Surrey with the Fringe on Top." And it was here that Loren bought a beautiful jade carving of prancing horses.

Two beautiful young girls, 17-year-old school dropouts in their national dress, acted as our guides through this wonderland. As educators, we were naturally concerned about them. But education seemed not to be as important here as in the eastern part of the country. From all we could see, the people do not seem to be very worried about it. They appear to be happy and carefree. Primarily immigrants from borderlands, their ethnic differences in culture and lifestyle make them a charming and unique people.

From ancient times, these agrarian people wanted and needed many children to help work the land. Further, the larger the family, the more prosperous a man was considered to be. In times past, men would have several wives, although this is not the practice today. Perhaps as the result of raising their own food and not depending entirely on the government to supply their livelihood, the people appear to be healthy and well fed.

Naturally, as our trip progressed, we visited the universities, where we were again offered positions. Loren was asked to teach at Yunnan University and I was offered a job at Kunming Normal College. What a temptation to come to such a warm and luxuriant place, far away from cold Dalian!

Yunnan University introduced us to two more "angels" who spent the day with us, leading us about. We gave them English names and they wrote to us later, begging us to come back to teach. We did not know it then, but it was not to be.

Our final destination was Guangzhou across the bay from Hong Kong. The rail system does not permit travel directly from Kunming to Guangzhou. Instead, travelers must backtrack and change trains at Changsha, which disappointed us somewhat at first. This two-day trip, however, took us through the most beautiful countryside we would see in China. Our train wandered through picturesque hills often depicted on Chinese porcelain, with terraced farmland beginning in the valleys and sometimes climbing up the steep sides of the mountains. The valleys were lush, the land resembling green patchwork quilts with blue lakes and sparkling streams full of fish. Our train wound in and out of tunnels, clinging to the sides of the hills, skirting lakes and crisscrossing rivers.

During this segment of our trip we shared our compartment with two gentlemen. The older man was reticent and seldom spoke or acknowledged us. But the younger man, who we guessed to be in his forties, was extremely curious about us.

Loren and I had made a practice of passing the tedious hours aboard the trains by playing endless games of Spite and Malice. Since the Chinese love card games, our compartment mate watched us closely hour after hour trying to discern what kind of game we were playing. The compartment offered nothing we could easily use as a card table. Though each compartment was fitted with one table, fastened to the wall under the window, this was filled with teacups, thermoses of hot water, and various items each of us wished to keep handy. Our American ingenuity again came into play.

Propping ourselves up with pillows at either end of our one lower bunk, we spread the thick, feather comforter across our laps, pulling it as tightly as possible to create a level playing area. Then we proceeded to play cards, to the amusement of our compartment mates. Hour after hour the younger man watched us from his upper bunk. We did not mind his avid attention to our card game. If we could have spoken Chinese, or if he had spoken English, perhaps we would have invited him to join us and taught him the game. What did bother me was the attention he gave me at other times.

When traveling with others in the compartment, Loren and I always slept in our clothing. If we needed to change clothes, we did so in the toilet where we were accustomed to sponge baths, washing our faces and hands in cold water, and brushing our teeth. The toilets were small and offered no bath facilities, but most disconcerting was the fact that the toilet itself emptied directly out onto the train tracks. There was no toilet paper. We learned to always carry our own. No toilets in China even remotely resembled those at home, most being trenches in the floor. At least those on the trains had seats.

The younger man watched me with fascination as I groomed myself, brushing my hair. His attention bothered me, making me squeamish and reticent. Though I tried to draw as little attention to myself as I could, it was impossible in such close quarters.

Early on the second day, shortly before we arrived in Changsha, we noticed the younger man writing feverishly. When the train entered the station and we prepared to disembark, he handed me a sealed envelope. What was written on the outside was in Chinese and I could not read it, so I slipped it into the pocket of my suitcase and forgot about it. After we returned to Dalian and unpacked, I rediscovered the letter and asked some of our students to interpret it for us. At first they were curious. Then they burst into laughter. It was a love letter! Our students never let me forget it.

We arrived in Changsha (Camellia City), our last stop, early in the morning before the ticket office opened. We needed to purchase tickets that day for the night train to Guangzhou and Hong Kong. As usual, the station was crowded with throngs of travelers. We tried to push our way through the crowds with no success, until one of the station guards motioned for us to sit on a bench outside the door. Repeatedly we tried to enter and make him understand what we wanted, but with no success. Each time we rose from the bench he angrily motioned for us to sit back down. Then, at 8:15 A.M., he called for us to follow him and, parting the crowds before us, led us to the front of the line before the ticket window just as it opened. Another "angel," a female student who spoke only faltering English, came to our aid, interpreting for us. By 8:25 we had our tickets for the night train to Guangzhou!

With a full day to enjoy, we checked our bags at a nearby hotel and set out to see the city. But we had no idea where to go or what to see. Two young women noticed our confusion and asked, "May we help you?" Two more "angels!" We gave them English names and, with Lisa and Julie to guide us, we started off for our day of adventure.

In a museum we saw the perfectly preserved body of a woman, perhaps an empress, taken from a tomb dating from 190 B.C. Here we also saw relics from the famous terra-cotta tombs of Xian. But the best thing we saw that day was the Temple in the Sky, a beautiful group of pavilions situated in a botanical garden.

There were three pavilions, or gates, to the temple. The first gate was a lovely place to sit and enjoy the garden. At the Drum Sounding Ridge, there was a stone bell like that at Anshan, which gave back beautiful melodies when it was struck. The second gate led us up marble steps toward the third gate, which was the actual entrance to the open-air temple. There we saw a very old, large bronze bell. Although it was not rung while we were there, we could imagine the beautiful tones it surely emitted. Again we remembered that "the rocks would cry out."

Most interesting of all was an ancient tree. The Chinese treasure and protect trees whose ages seem to defy the laws of nature. This small tree, as gnarled and crooked as an old man, dated from the fourteenth century. How it had survived and lived so long seemed a miracle and a mystery.

The flowers were lush and in full bloom. We wandered through the rose garden snapping pictures and enjoying the lovely fragrances. Here we saw Chinese musicians playing on instruments foreign to us. The music they make is hauntingly beautiful and is uniquely Chinese! It was a lovely day, and we learned why this is called Camellia City.

In the evening as we waited for our train, we took our two "angels" out to dinner. I was wearing the sweatshirt my friend Joan sent me for Christmas, on which she had embroidered the words *God Bless My Special Friend.*

"Do you believe in God?" they asked.

It was an open door. We talked to them about God, the Creation, and Redemption. We told them about prayer and that they were an answer to ours. Through wonder and tears, they experienced the love we had come to bring. The guards allowed them to wait with us in the soft-sleeper waiting room and to come all the way with us to the door of the train. They wept as they told us good-bye, begging us to return. Our prayer was that God would send others in answer to their pleas.

We spent the following days in Hong Kong at our conference and with Dan and his family in Thailand swimming in the South China Sea.

It was hot! It was wonderful! And it was over too soon.

18

China Joy

"Joy means the perfect fulfillment of that for which I was created and regenerated, not the successful doing of a thing."—Oswald Chambers

It was late February and very cold when we returned to Dalian. Thoughts of balmy days and sunny beaches tugged at our memories. Would we ever be happy again in Dalian? Would the dirty, icy wind off the Gobi Desert chill the excitement we had experienced in the past few weeks? Did God *really* want us in this frigid land? We had been called. We had answered. We had committed ourselves. The rest was up to Him. And He never fails His children.

As we walked back onto the campus in cold Dalian, we somehow felt as though spring was in the air. Such a surge of joy welled up in us that we knew we were where we were supposed to be. Shortly after returning we read in Oswald Chamber's book *My Utmost for His Highest* that "joy means the perfect fulfillment of that for which I was created and regenerated, not the successful doing of a thing." God had been preparing us our entire lives for this time, and the joy was so strong we almost burst with it. It really didn't matter where we were as long as He had brought us there.

Our students greeted us with so much love that we wondered how we could have ever been tempted to leave them. But I soon discovered I had a problem.

"My face really hurts," I complained. "It's always aching when I come back from class."

Loren gave me a quizzical look.

"Don't you know why?" he asked in disbelief.

"No! Why? If something's wrong, why didn't you tell me?" I scolded.

"I'll tell you why," he said laughing. "It's because you go around with that crazy grin on your face all the time!"

So that was it! He was always smiling too. But that was usually natural for him, so it had never registered. It was the joy! We were bursting with it! Soon we began to see wonderful things happen.

The frigid temperatures could do nothing to chill the joy and warmth in our hearts. In fact, we would have more snow, which was an answer to prayer. For the second year, China was in the midst of drought. Though we complained about the lack of water when it was turned off for hours and sometimes days at a time, it was a necessary measure because of the drought conditions. After spending time in Thailand and Malaysia where everything was green and lush, the terrible natural conditions in China seemed even more evident to us, and we began to pray for rain.

During one class, our lesson touched on the bogs in northern England, and I had to explain to the students about ground so saturated with rain that it became unstable. Referring to the dry conditions around us, I mentioned that I had been praying for rain. When we came out of the building after class, a light mist had begun which turned into heavier showers in the evening. One of our students called us later, unable to contain her excitement.

"Mom," she cried, "look outside! It's raining, just as you said. You told us you were praying for rain, and now it's raining. God answered your prayer!"

We never knew when some little thing would make a big impression and touch their hearts with the message of the power of God.

Spring brought a beauty to Dalian that we had not seen before. An outing to a park located at the foot of a dam to the reservoir supplying Dalian's water provided us with fascinating snapshots of China's people. The park's cherry trees exploded with blooms. We spread our picnic on the ground and watched the throngs of people around us. One young woman, with plaited hair hanging to her knees, captivated us, so striking was her appearance. After getting a fleeting look at her, she disappeared into the crowd. It was unusual to see any Chinese woman with long hair. During the Cultural Revolution, most women were encouraged to wear mannish pantsuits and cut their hair. With bobbed hair and boxy suits, Chinese society had taken on a unisex appearance.

In our wanderings on the paths of the lovely park, I was distracted, constantly on the lookout for the young woman and her magnificent hair. Finally, near sunset, we came upon her in the midst of a small group of women.

"Would you mind," I asked through an interpreter, "if we take your picture?"

Gracious and smiling, she turned about, allowing us to film that wondrous braid which swung gently against her knees. Finding her at last had made my day.

Schoolchildren, wild on a holiday out of school and full of fun, also caught our attention that day. Admonished to stay together in a group, instead they were all over the place, as most children anywhere would be. They scampered up the sides of the spillway of the dam and gave grief to the distraught teachers attempting to herd them. Double trouble came in the form of twin boys, double happiness to the Chinese.

Elderly couples rested on benches under the cherry trees, which showered them with fragrance as the blossoms drifted down like snow. The women, their tiny feet tucked demurely beneath their gowns, displayed a natural modesty, not wanting us to stare at their "golden lilies." Tempted to photograph such a rare sight, I refrained from doing so since it would have offended the women.

They had been children of an age whose practice was to break and bind the feet of small girls. According to history, this painful practice, originally instituted to prevent wives from straying, became the sign of high-born women who, through necessity, were rendered incapable of performing even the smallest tasks and were cared for by others all their lives. This mutilation of girls' feet was forbidden in the early 1900s and women with "golden lilies" are seldom seen in public today.

That spring also provided us with an opportunity to go fishing. One of our students who had access to a car and driver took us along the coast where we went out in a small fishing boat into the bay. Loren, who loved to fish, caught nothing. But our friend's 11-year-old son caught fish, which he gave to us.

Trolling with our lines, we tied into something which we had trouble landing at first. Pulling up our catch, we found we had unintentionally robbed someone's trotline of a large catch of shellfish. Having been warned not to eat fresh fish from the bay because of the danger of hepatitis, we passed this delicious catch on to friends who were not so fearful. We were quite sure we had often been fed local fish in the restaurants, but we nevertheless were not ready to tempt fate and serve it to ourselves.

130

Eager to entertain us, our Department of Foreign Affairs took us on an exciting trip to the International Kite Festival in Weifang. We traveled overnight by boat, then by train, before arriving at our destination in the Shandong Province.

Our first evening in Weifang found us at a lovely little park for the Lantern Festival, where we saw beautiful Chinese lanterns in many sizes and shapes, as well as displays from famous Chinese classics. We would have purchased a lantern to take home, but for some reason they did not seem to be a tourist item. Nowhere could we find one for sale. The following day we attended the opening ceremonies of the kite festival and wandered through the kite museum full of beautiful kites from large dragons, hundreds of feet long, to tiny intricate birds and butterflies. At a visit to the kite factory, we watched the kite makers in action. We wanted to encourage our students to build their own kites and have a kite-flying contest, so we took back kites for them to fly. They preferred to buy rather than build their kites, but none were available in Dalian, so Loren had to teach them how to build a kite. In the vicinity of the kite factory we had the opportunity to see the ancient art of block printing: carved blocks, each dipped into a different color of ink. As we watched, we noticed one old gentleman actually carving the blocks to use in the printing.

An interesting sideline of this trip was a tour through ancient homes of ruling lords. Some had been well preserved and were open to tourists. Our Foreign Affairs hosts delighted in taking our picture in the Wedding Chamber of the Rich Man's House. Most of the trappings had been preserved including two wedding carts, one for the groom decorated in blue, and one for the bride decorated in red. In

China, instead of white, the color for the bridal dress is red or bright pink, or sometimes a combination of these two colors.

The city of Weifang provided fantastic entertainment. We spent two nights at a large stadium where we witnessed a magnificent parade and the opening festivities. Thousands of schoolchildren in colorful uniforms paraded, danced, and performed intricate drills on the field. Something exciting was happening everywhere we looked. Kite clubs from all over the world, including several from America, paraded in colorful carts. We were thrilled to see the Stars and Stripes flying above some of the most magnificent kites in the show.

On our last day in Weifang, we went to a large level flying field where hundreds of people had gathered to fly their kites. The day was lovely and the activities exciting to watch, especially as most of the kites were in the shapes of birds, butterflies, or animals. Perhaps the most unusual kites were those of dragons several hundred feet long. From a great distance before arriving at the field, we could see kites flying so high and so long that their tails fell back to earth, their arches resembling the Arch in St. Louis.

Everywhere we went we seemed to draw a crowd. Those who came to watch the kites ended up watching us instead. We were fortunate to have as guides and interpreters English teachers from the middle (high) school in Weifang. One lovely young woman Loren named Wendy. Early in the day she had asked him to describe himself. Perhaps it was because she was interested in teaching descriptive writing in her English classes. Jokingly he said, "I am rich, powerful, and handsome." That got quite a laugh, but not as much as the retelling of it did later.

Loren loved to take pictures, and our young teacher-guides were willing subjects. As he wrote his address for some of the young teachers, we looked up to discover that a large crowd of curious Chinese had surrounded us. Soon cameras began to snap as the Chinese turned the tables on us and took our pictures. We took little notice until an older gentleman with a very professional-looking camera began to take our pictures. After he had finished, he spoke briefly to Wendy and left. When he was gone, Loren asked her what had transpired.

"He is the editor of the local newspaper. He is doing a front-page article for tomorrow's edition," she replied.

"What did you tell him about us?" Loren asked.

"I told him you were rich, powerful, and handsome," she said.

We all laughed as Loren stood with egg on his face!

Our students loved hearing this story when we told them about it after returning home. When the newspaper came out, Wendy clipped the picture and article and sent it to us. Loren was never able to live down the story anymore than I could live down my Chinese love letter. It only made our students love him more.

On our last evening in Weifang, we returned to the stadium for an elaborate fireworks display, a natural thing to do, since the Chinese invented fireworks. Many Foreign Experts attended the festival, and we all seemed to be seated together. We were excited about the show and could not fathom the stoical Chinese who never smiled, cheered, or showed any emotion at the beautiful display. Perhaps they were accustomed to it.

Most of the Foreign Experts were quite young. Loren and I suspected that we must have been the oldest in China! But we caught the spirit of our American friends who began to give football cheers for the city of Weifang for putting on such a magnificent show for us. The stadium held perhaps 10,000 people that evening, but only the crazy *Meiguowens* (Americans) cheered the show, causing others to turn and look at us as if they couldn't understand what we were so excited about. Our seats, directly behind the band, afforded us perfect opportunities to sing along as they played nonstop throughout the evening. Every other song seemed to be "Oh! Susanna." The Chinese seem to really love American music.

We boarded the Iron Rooster for our trip home at 2:00 in the morning, expecting to fall into our nice, reserved soft-sleeper bunks. But, as usual in China, since we were not onboard by bedtime, our compartments had been given to others whose cheaper, hard-seat or hard-sleeper tickets had been upgraded. This usually meant that a little "dough" had greased the palms of the attendants and our berths had been sold again.

So, as there was nothing else to do, we spent the remainder of the night sitting in the dining car. We wouldn't have missed it for the world! The sleepier we got, the crazier we became, and the entire party indulged in one bout of laughter after another. Our train was one of the newer ones, but something must have been wrong with the brakes (or the brake operator). Every time the train slowed coming into a station, the brakes jammed, throwing trays of dishes onto the floor. Time after time the cooks patiently swept up the broken crockery, appearing to think nothing of it. The only ones it seemed to faze were the foreigners and their hosts, who fell into fits of laughter as we were tossed about along with the dishes, almost tumbling into the floor with the shattered china.

Tired but happy, we disembarked at Yantai, also known as Old Chefoo and the site where Hudson Taylor had established his headquarters for the China Inland Mission in the 1860s. It was here that he built a rest area for his people, as well as a boarding school and hospital. We understood that its remains are still there today, although we were not taken to see them. Instead, our hosts were only interested in showing us Chinese antiquities, old palaces, and Buddhist temples. Our next stop was at Penglai, a lovely little fishing village on the coast. It is also a tourist attraction for Christians, for it is the former home and church of Lottie Moon, an early Baptist missionary. There we also visited elaborate summer palaces and enjoyed warm, balmy weather.

Our year seemed to be coming to a rapid close, but we believed that we would return the next year. God had called us to China, and as Paul said, we cannot be "disobedient unto the heavenly vision" (Acts 26:19 KJV). We were just now really beginning to see things progress.

◆

By spring, I was teaching 18 hours, 2 of these without assigned materials. I was told I could teach anything I wished. The American English literature books originally assigned had opened with fable, folklore, and fantasy short stories. So now the novel seemed to be an appropriate choice. I chose to teach C. S. Lewis's *The Lion, the Witch and the Wardrobe.*

With no student books available, each week I typed and handed out two or three chapters from my own copy of the book. It was a wonderful experience for the students who at first considered it a "baby book," but who began to understand the different levels of meaning in the allegory. Soon they came to see the symbolic meaning of each character and the overall theme of the story. It was a thrill to see looks of wonder as the truth began to dawn on them and they came to understand its deeper meaning. I promised never to test them on it; but a greater Teacher than I would do that. It was getting more exciting all the time!

The joy and wonder of being in China never left us. We were getting to know our students and they were beginning to open to our teaching. So we were gratified when we were informed that we had been invited back for another year. We had known for some time that we were meant to be there longer, but now it was official. We *knew* where we were supposed to be the next winter. As long as our hearts were right and our spirits were so sure, we knew we must be in Dalian. There was still so much to do. It would be sad to leave when things were just beginning. We were in the Lord's hands and He was beginning to work His perfect will for us in China.

We learned to say with Paul: "None of these things move me, neither count I my life dear unto myself, so that I might finish my course with joy, and the ministry which I have received from the Lord Jesus, to testify the gospel of the grace of God" (Acts 20:24 KJV).

In the months to come, this could truly be said of Loren.

The day was lovely and long. It was one of the last really carefree days we had in China.

19

Tiananmen Square: Losing Heaven's Mandate

It was spring. Everything in Dalian should have been beautiful. But we found ourselves looking at our world through tears. By the middle of April our hearts broke as we watched China move toward crisis. The country was in revolt.

Deng Xiaoping had introduced economic reforms in the 1970s. He wanted to modernize China, but he had not envisioned a loss of his power when he launched such reforms in direct contradiction with the Communist ideology. His hard, Communist mind, upon instituting the government's new austerity program, could not foresee that freedom would bring independent thought and defiance of the party line. Communism had proclaimed the right of the people to throw off the rule of the emperors and the ruling class, to make everyone equal. Power should lie with the people. Such freedom, it was said, was a mandate from heaven. The event that triggered the revolt was the death of Hu Yaobang, the ousted

Communist Party leader who had advocated reforms in government and who, in death, had become something of a martyr.

Our Christian witness had been slow at first, for during the first semester we just tried to feel our way and get acquainted. But after our return in the spring, things began to accelerate. Those students closest to us seemed hungriest for the good news we had come to bring them. As sunshine seems more brilliant shining through dark banks of clouds, so the moving of the Spirit seemed extremely bright to us.

Our first inclination of the approaching storm was the copious amounts of posters pasted on every available wall space on the campus. Going to and from class we passed groups of students clustered about, avidly reading the messages. Since we could not read Chinese, we could only inquire from others their contents. Hesitant to say much, our students revealed to us that the posters were political. They warned us not to become involved. Then our students, like students all over China, went on strike. They began boycotting classes on May 18. There had been a massive rally with other university students in the town square. The day the strike began, we went to class to find our classrooms empty.

Hearing voices outside, I went to the window and looked out to see what seemed to be the entire student body lined up in marching order. They were ready to parade downtown to join other university students in protest. They were excited and there was a restless air of expectation about them as they mobilized.

Seeing me at the window, they waved and shouted, and called for me to join them. Other teachers had done so. But as excited as I was for their enthusiasm, there was within me that still, small voice Who said, "Careful! Don't go. This is not your fight. This is not why I brought you here."

So I smiled at them and waved them on, giving them my blessing. They wanted to be free and were determined to do whatever it took to be so. At the head of the line, smiling and waving happily, begging me to join her, was Barbara. One of the brightest students in the university, Barbara had been monitor of Loren's classes first semester, and now served as monitor of mine. Her quick mind and sweet spirit had made it easy to become fond of her. She was loyal. She was dependable. She was there for us when things puzzled us and we needed clarification. She had a good Chinese mind. In other words, she was good at logic and reasoning. Faith she could not comprehend. It was not within her ability to accept by faith things she could neither see nor reason out. We loved her dearly, but we could not touch her spirit. It was disappointing to fail with the best. And she was the best. And she *thought* she was going to Beijing!

As American teachers, we were aware that our students hungered for freedom. What we were not aware of was that there was growing dissatisfaction all over China with the corrupt government. We believed that the unrest had come partly from our students' association with us. Coming to China to teach them English, we had been encouraged to tell them about life in America. They heard about freedom from us and they wanted it. We believed we had perverted them!

The morning had been beautiful, but by night thunderclouds rolled in from the sea and drenching rains soaked the students resolved to cling together in the city square. They were determined to go to Beijing, joining other college students from all over

China. As the turbulent night moved around us, a soft knock at our door revealed Barbara, wet and weeping. She had chosen to come to us rather than go to the capital. We wrapped her, disillusioned, chilled, and shaking, in warm blankets and filled her with hot soup and tea until her shaking ceased. The Lord, in some way, had prevented her from joining that fateful march. I know now that He had good things in store for her, and Satan was not allowed to pervert His plans.

The students had intended only a peaceful "strike" in Tiananmen Square before the house of government.

They would talk to the leaders.

They would ask for a loosening of control on their lives.

They would talk against the corruption and nepotism in the government.

They would ask for a rise in the standard of living.

They only wanted to talk.

At first, the old men were courteous, inviting some of the young people into the government palace to confer. In their naive and childish ignorance, the students were plied with tea and beguiling smiles. Those who went were identified as troublemakers and, without knowing what they did, brought suspicion upon themselves. They put themselves in harm's way and their days were numbered. But the whole world would soon know what happened.

Party Chief Zhao Ziyang, believing in the people's right to express themselves, had allowed the press to cover the student movement. The scene in Beijing was televised across China and around the world. Television, radio, and newspapers were filled with sympathetic accounts of the students' peaceful protest. It was becoming a new day for China.

But the sun quickly set on that new day. Having heard all their pleas, and finally losing patience with the outspoken youth, Deng Xiaoping declared martial law; and the tanks roared into Tiananmen Square, crushing the protest, killing hundreds and wounding thousands, destroying everything in their path in full view of Chinese television and the international press. Then all news was blacked out. But it was too late. The people of China and the world had heard and seen enough to know the truth.

Our students were there, and those who escaped came back with horror stories of death and carnage of fellow students who had nothing to fight back with except sticks and stones. One student related how, asleep in a tent, he was awakened by the roar of the tanks. Peering out and seeing the impending doom, he escaped just in time. Others in the tent were not so fortunate. They were trapped as the monstrous machines of death rolled over them, leaving their lifeless bodies behind.

We were never to know which of our students were killed and which students, alive but with a price on their heads, had fled and gone into hiding, fearful of being hunted down as rebels by the government. Returning to the campus, one student attempted to share his traumatic experience with others. But he was soon hushed, and never again did we hear him relate his story.

There were those like Barbara who had remained on campus. But as the days passed and news of the massacre at Tiananmen began to filter through, many of the remaining students packed their meager belongings and left school for the safety of their homes. Finally, word came that the military would be invading our campus. It was not clear what the purpose of this action was, but we saw the results of this rumor. "We are seeing history made today," we wrote. We stood on the balcony of the guesthouse and watched as a stream of students flowed silently in single file down the hilly pathway of the campus and out the gate to catch the trains, making their way to the safety of their homes.

It was amazing how much we had come to love our students. Calling us Mom and Dad as they would never have dared address their Chinese teachers, they had become more than students to us. They were our dear Chinese children. We wept to see them go. They waved timidly to us as they passed, and we waved back, wondering if we would ever see them again. Shirley was among them.

Shirley came to us in tears the night before she left, bringing us a gift she had intended to give us at the anniversary party some of the students and faculty had planned for us. The sweet porcelain figure of Dutch children sits in my kitchen window now, a constant reminder of this dear student. One of the other teachers commented that she felt Shirley might harm herself, so distraught was she. When Shirley came to say good-bye, her depression was obvious. There seemed no hope for the future. China had reverted to the dark days of the Cultural Revolution. There appeared to be nowhere for this generation to turn. All seemed lost. But I knew Who held Shirley's future in His hand.

"How long is your train trip home?" I asked.

"Three days in a hard-seat coach," she shuddered.

"Will you do something for me?" I asked.

"Of course," she replied, attempting to smile.

Comforting her as best I could, I put a Gospel of John in her hands. "On your trip home, will you read this little book?"

She nodded numbly, stuffing it into her satchel. Putting my arms around her, we stood silent for a moment as I prayed for her, then I bid her good-bye, believing I would never see or hear from her again.

But the Lord requires of us only that we plant seed. It is He Who causes it to sprout and grow and ripen into fruit.

Three days later the phone rang. It was Shirley.

"Mom," she shouted joyfully, "I've been born again!"

Only in the Gospel of John had she seen the words *born again.* On that long train ride home the Holy Spirit had taken the seed and sown it in her heart, bringing her new life and hope for the future. China is not lost as long as the Word is there.

Although most of the students had gone and the campus was deserted, Loren and I continued to go to our classrooms. The doors were locked and we could not get in; but as is the rule for classes and professors in America, we waited for 10 minutes each hour before returning home. President Li, the Communist Party chief, and our own dear Foreign Affairs friends watched us walk past the administration building each hour and sent word that it was not necessary for us to continue the vigil. Other teachers had ceased to haunt the halls of the deserted classroom buildings. But we could not.

"Why do you go when you know no one will come?" asked President Li.

"We signed a contract. We are obligated to be there whether the students come or not," was Loren's answer. We continued to make our way across campus day after day.

We were able to get no news of Beijing on Chinese television after a government censorship was imposed and both Voice of America and the British

Broadcasting Company broadcasts were jammed. Our families at home had more news than we had. The evening news showed films (which had been smuggled out) of the carnage. Rosanna's parents called almost nightly, relating the latest information from American television and pleading with her to come home. There was the mop up when the nameless bodies of the dead students, piled together and burned in mass, sent up flames and smoke without any records of who they were. The majority of the people in China were unable to learn any more truth about what was happening. They only knew that many of their sons and daughters never came home again. They were either dead or running for their lives.

On June 14 we left Dalian with many other westerners who had come from all over Manchuria for an airlift provided by the Canadian government. President Bush strongly encouraged all United States citizens to get out of China. Since our embassy had little or no power to protect us, and since we seemed highly aligned with the students and their desire for freedom, it was most expedient for us to leave. It seemed wrong for us to do so. We knew in our hearts our work was not done. But the Lord knew what was going on in our lives and He was in charge. All we could do was be prudent and go as we had been requested to do.

The day before our exit will be forever engraved upon my mind and heart. It was one of the most poignant days of the entire year. Our students filled our little apartment. They came to say good-bye, but stayed to grieve with us over our leaving. Emotions were running high and our fellowship was that of a family soon to be parted, perhaps never to see one another again.

Among these was Leon. He was an exceptional young man, a brilliant mathematics scholar who was already teaching lower division math classes. He had been allowed to skip some of his own classes, doing his work on his own time, in order to audit my class. Slow at opening up at first, he suddenly became eager. One of the greatest compliments I was to receive in China came from him.

"Mom," he said, "you taught me more than English. You taught me how to love my own mother."

The morning of our evacuation began with a heavy downpour. President Li and our Communist Party friend came to the lobby of the guesthouse to tell us good-bye and see us board the van that would take us to the airport. Standing with parting gifts in their hands, they gave us the greatest gift of all, a gift from the heart. Many universities had expelled their American teachers, asking them never to return, blaming them for the unrest and dissatisfaction in the hearts of the youth. Not ours.

"Come back," they pleaded. "We have never had anyone love our young people the way you do." We knew, as they did not, that it was really God pouring out His love for China through us.

We boarded the large van along with as many of our students as could crowd in. It was a wet day, both inside and outside the bus, as we wept because of the separation that was coming. At the airport, crowded with other westerners who had come to fly out with us, we huddled in our own little group, arms too short to encircle everyone we yearned to touch and embrace. Loren did a shocking thing. Approaching Xiuzhen, the young Foreign Affairs official who was no older than our own daughter but who had become one of our dearest friends and staunchest supporters, he lightened the soberness of the moment and brought laughter into the gloom.

"I'm going to kiss you good-bye," he said to the startled woman.

Extremely shy and not accustomed to shows of affection in public, she drew away momentarily.

Loren and Xiuzhen had come a long way since the early days when he sat patiently near her desk awaiting the arrival of the old trunk.

Our students were ecstatic. As they held their breaths, he planted a tender, loving kiss on her dear cheek.

"Now," he said, pointing to his own dimpled cheek, "I want you to kiss me."

And she returned the kiss to the delight of all who knew how much we loved her.

The last picture in our minds that day was of our little group standing at the gate weeping, tears streaming down their faces as they waved good-bye. We left them completely alone and with the full knowledge that they could very well be the objects of political harassment, interrogation, or even persecution because of their closeness to their Western teachers.

Our first week in China I had written the lines which became so meaningful.

> Oh, Lord, I leave it gladly all behind,
> The home I love, my children running free.
> Eternal things hang balanced in Your hand.
> I touch the scales for China and for Thee.

Now we longed to know if we had really touched the scales, if what we had done had mattered. We had planted seed. It was well watered with the tears we shed that day. But the Holy Spirit is the Gardener and the reaping of the harvest is for Him. It will be in eternity that we will know the full measure, pressed down and running over, of the harvest of our beloved students that we left behind that day.

20

Har Shalom

"God's work, done in God's way, will never lack God's supplies."—Hudson Taylor

We were at home at Har Shalom (Hill of Peace) on the shores of the lake in eastern Oklahoma. It had never been our intent to come out of China the summer after our first year. We would stay and travel. We would see parts of China we had missed on our other sight-seeing trips. But the massacre in Tiananmen Square changed all of that.

Instead of seeing China, when we left in mid-June we went through Hong Kong and Egypt on our way to Israel, where we joined our son Steve and his family for a month's holiday in England and Switzerland. We had a summer to spend, and we planned to see beautiful places we had never seen before. After our European holiday was over, we planned to go home, see the rest of the family, restock supplies, take our physicals, and return to China for our second year at Dongbei.

The Foreign Affairs Office at our university had insisted that we apply for reentry visas, believing that by fall tensions would lessen and we would be allowed to return. In our latest communication we were assured that we were "warmly welcomed back." With less than a month to go, and with our tickets tucked safely away, we were in the frantic mode of packing for our return to China. Without the wonderful old trunk, Loren was in the process of building boxes to ship our household supplies and books. Happy and excited, with that familiar China joy bubbling up inside of us, we went for the necessary physical checkups. Loren seemed to be in excellent health, but as a precautionary measure, he was given a CAT scan.

"You mustn't go," admonished the doctor. "We found more activity. You have a new tumor."

"I feel fine!" Loren declared. "We have our tickets. Our boxes and bags are packed. They are expecting us! We must go!" he insisted.

Loren was usually determined when he had made up his mind, and his mind was made up. He was going back to China!

"Not now," the doctor reiterated. "Maybe later if there is no significant change."

"Doc," Loren said, "you had better get your best shots in now because after that we're going back."

So we notified Foreign Affairs that we could not come immediately because of a "family" problem.

Loren began to undergo his treatments, but a necessary second series of testing would not come until October. By that time it would be too late to return for the fall semester.

Again we wired China.

"Please allow us to return next fall," we requested, praying that this was only a temporary setback.

It grieved us to leave our students, our new "lambs." Our deepest concern was that the Good Shepherd would send others to teach and nourish them. Only the brightest middle (high) school graduates, the top 2 percent of Chinese young people, are admitted to college. The education is free to those who qualify under such stringent quotas. It was this level of society, the intelligentsia, which had never before been reached with the gospel. The rural underground church, the simple, country people, had embraced Christianity for years. Even during the Cultural Revolution, when persecution was the worst, the spark had not gone out. This segment of the church was growing rapidly. But to these simple people, the upper level of society was suspect. It was there that the Communist Party had been the strongest.

Now God was reaching out to those who had never been touched before. He was doing it by bringing into the universities of China Christian teachers who not only taught English but brought the love of God with them.

We had heard God's call. We had been obedient. We had gone on faith. We had ministered the word. Now we waited at home, not knowing what would happen to our students.

We know the Holy Spirit can and does teach. But as the Ethiopian eunuch cried out to Philip, "How can I understand unless someone helps me?" we yearned for them to receive proper guidance. He had called us. He would call others.

However, the Holy Spirit was already doing God's work God's way. In the days and weeks to come, we received word that showed us that the broken ground was being plowed and weeded and harrowed, as new seed fell into the hungry earth.

Letters from those we left behind in China began to pour in.

"Dear Friends:" wrote Xiuzhen. "One month and a half has passed since you left Dalian for your home country. I miss you very much. I never forget the days when we were together. I often think of you. Every day I can't help looking at the photos we took. It seems I hear your voice and we are talking happily."

It was Diana who cried out:

"So often we recalled the poem period when you taught us. After you went back, we were just like children who have lost their parents."

Donna wrote, after returning home, about how the Lord touched her.

"The morning before Virginia and I were going home, we talked only a little, but the book you gave me influenced me very much. You all have such a deep belief in God and love each other so deeply.

"Those days I was just confused about the meaning of life. Why couldn't I believe in God? Only we have been taught that there is no God for almost 20 years. It's impossible for me to believe in God overnight.

"So I will read the book you gave me. I still have a long way to go in order to search for the key to the mysteries of the universe and the meaning of life. I love the words you've told us, the lessons you've taught us."

"Thank you for your lessons!

"Thank you for your encouragement!

"Please come back to China!"

For Donna, it was our prayer that, with her searching mind, the Lord would find His way into her heart.

From Virginia we heard this:

"Thank God for sending you with us.

"Thanks for the love you showed with us.

"I got crazy about reading the Bible.

"I have a piece of wonderful news to share with you. I have been made a member of a big family full of love. I'm now a Christian. I've been baptized. I can hardly describe how much love I get from God. He fills my heart with love and makes me love others. Now I can understand why you look so happy, so beautiful, so young for your age, why your marriage is so successful. That is because the love of God lives in your hearts making you be united as one flesh. And your love comes out to others naturally. How wonderful all these things are.

"I love God with all my heart, soul, mind, and strength. I know it is Him Who sent you with us. It's a pity that I appreciated it so late. I got so much love from you, but I failed to give that much to you, though I wanted to.

"Although I am aware whether you'll return or not is God's arrangement, I still hope from the bottom of my heart that God can make you be with us again. Do you feel your students on the other shore of the ocean are expecting you back eagerly and strongly? Be back, dear teachers! We love you and miss you.

"Dear teachers, no matter whether you are back or not, my love and prayers will always be with you.

"It was you who sowed seeds of love in my heart, though you didn't wait for the time to see the seeds sprout and bloom and fruit. God knows all you've done, and I know it in my heart, too.

"Thank you for bringing love to my world."

Leon, that dear young man who came lately to us, was heartbroken. We could almost see his tears

152

through the beauty of the poetry pouring from his heart.

"Dear Mom and Dad: Our campus is calmed now, but my heart is not calmed. I'm terribly upset. I'm tired of everything. But I don't think this emptiness of my heart will last long.

"Only the Bible can give me the feeling of holy and pure. At dusk, when I close the Bible, looking out the window, seeing the glow of the setting sun, I feel that God is great. Or some afternoons after swimming, lying on the beach, watching the wide sky and the endless seas, I couldn't help reciting, 'Our Father in heaven, hallowed be Your name.' At that moment, my heart was filled with solemn silence.

"One night I dreamed of meeting you at the gate of the campus. Papa and you were back, carrying two big suitcases. As soon as Mom caught sight of me, she laid down her suitcase and ran to me, crying out, 'Leon! Leon!' Oh, I was in such a happy astonishment that I nearly cried.

"Mom! Daddy! Leon prays for you back!"

Most comforting of all was the reassurance from Eugene, that wonderful soul in whom God had placed a missionary heart.

"Dear Mom and Dad: Now I graduated and arranged to work in Shanghai. I am not satisfied with it, but I take it as God's arrangement, for God causes all things to work together for good.

"I want to study theology. I wish God will use me to work for Him. Let's pray for the Lord to give us wisdom and to be zealous for His work. Also, pray for me that I should bear fruit for the Lord.

"Grace and peace to you from God the Father and the Lord Jesus Christ.

"Emmanuel!"

Eugene was learning with Paul, just as we were "in whatsoever state I am, therewith to be content" (Phil. 4:11 KJV).

Hudson Taylor, founder of the China Inland Mission in the 1860s, said, "God's work, done in God's way, will never lack God's supplies."

With yearning hearts, we prayed that the work He started so simply through us would be nourished and protected, truly bringing forth fruit worthy of the harvest.

21

Aslan Is on the Move

"God's gifts and his call are irrevocable" (Rom. 11:29 NIV).

Years ago God had put China in our hearts. He had called us there. Satan had tried to thwart His plans, but he was powerless. The stalemate was over. We were going back.

In February we packed our suitcases and boxes. In our hearts was excitement and the anticipation of once more being able to share the good news of God's love with the young people we loved so much.

We had weathered our frustration and disappointment at not being able to return in the fall. Chinese hearts had been open and eager and very receptive to the word of the Lord. Only the Father knew the reason we were stopped at the last moment by Loren's lymphoma. We delayed our return one semester in order to give the doctors their chance. But after seven months nothing had changed. Loren's only illness seemed to come from the chemotherapy.

"We might as well have been in China," he reasoned.

"You are going back with a loaded gun at your head," the doctor warned.

But it was time to go back.

When we wired our Foreign Affairs Office asking for official permission to return the following fall, back came an urgent reply, much like that from the man of Macedonia, "Come now!"

So we renewed our tickets and set our faces toward China.

The news from China was not too encouraging. Friends returning warned that we must anticipate stricter conditions and less association with the students. However, as in most situations where there is a degree of suppression and persecution, the report was that the young people were coming to the Lord in large numbers. Baptisms were numerous, and the famine of faith under Communism had whetted the spiritual appetite of the people. They were crying out for hope. They were thirsting for the good news.

Although many doors seemed to have closed, others were opening miraculously and the work of the Holy Spirit was abounding. C. S. Lewis fans rejoiced with us when our friend Joan related that her pastor had declared from the pulpit, "Aslan is on the move!" The Lion of Judah was roaring through China.

When doubt began to creep in with words of caution from friends and loved ones, the Word came in to strengthen us. Steve confirmed our decision to return when he gave us Romans 11:29 (NIV): "God's gifts and his call are irrevocable."

He had called.

We had answered.

Satan tried to stop us, but we would not be stopped. Only God could do that.

We stepped out on faith to return to the work God had called us to do.

We were going back.

So on a blustery day in February we boarded an Air China 747 to return to China.

We landed in Shanghai in a snowstorm, but the snow was a welcoming sign to us. Its purity seemed to cover the awful stains of the previous spring.

There was still the matter of clearing customs. Again the Lord was with us. The "angel" he sent was an unlikely ally. But it was Loren's great sense of humor that helped carry us through.

At the customs table sat four very stern-looking officials. Bright and crisp in their uniforms, with a strong air of authority about them, they gave us pause. As usual, we prayed fervently. Then the Lord brought our "angel" to our rescue.

For some mysterious reason we were never to know, our luggage was to be loaded onto scales to be weighed before being opened. It was the task of a worker, a small and fiery woman, to handle the bags. There seemed to be some sort of friction between her and the officials, for the tone of the conversation was snappish. Whatever they were saying to her must have been abrasive, for it was causing her to react angrily.

Loren, always the tease, egged her on in her rebuttal with her superiors, although he had no idea what was being said. The more they antagonized her, the louder became her response. Filled with excitement born of apprehension, we laughed. The more she responded, the more Loren encouraged her. The more he encouraged her, the more we laughed with pure joy at the verbal battle that was raging around us, a spiritual battle that we sensed the Lord was winning.

Finally, exasperated by the officials, and spurred on by Loren's encouragement, the tiny woman appeared to say, "Mess with me, will you? I'll take the bags outside right now!"

Evidencing no fear of her superiors, our "angel" carried our bags, not to the examining tables, but out the exit door and gave them to the taxi driver who took us to the airport, laughing all the way. This time, the Lord's "angel" had been a tiny, laughing woman. She had "delivered" us.

We flew to Dalian through the frigid, starless night. As the only foreigners aboard the small plane, we felt the suspicious glances and cold stares of the other passengers. For some reason their resentment of us was almost palatable. But they were soon in for a shock. Although we traveled east through the cold, dark Chinese sky, we arrived in Dalian to warm hugs, arms and hearts open wide, and shouts of joy.

Our friends from the Foreign Affairs Office were waiting for us this time. To the surprise of the other passengers, the stoical Chinese who seemed not happy to have shared their night flight with us, we raced into the warm airport terminal and were instantly engulfed with laughter. Xiuzhen, our precious friend, ran to me. In each other's arms, we danced and whirled about as the astonished Chinese looked on. Important government officials had come to meet us, shattering our fellow passengers' disdain of us.

We did not care. We were home!

Carried joyously to our old rooms at the Foreign Experts Guesthouse, we deposited our luggage and unpacked our bags. All of our old household belongings were where we had left them. Although we had been gone for the entire fall semester, it seemed as though we had hardly been gone at all. Nothing had changed.

Still experiencing jet lag, we found it hard to settle down. Donning our coats against the bitter night, we went to the dormitory where our students had lived the year before, praying that they were still there. And, of course, they were.

Not allowed to go upstairs to the students' rooms, we were permitted to call them on the house phone. Hearing our voices must have been a shock. At first they questioned who we *really* were, a verification which must come from those in charge of the dorm. Even more surprising to them was the fact that we were actually downstairs in the office. Sweet Veronica, who was in the process of washing her hair, rushed down the stairs and into our arms, her wet head wrapped in a towel. It was the homecoming we had dreamed it would be. We were not disappointed.

And then there was Barbara.

Coming to us with joy, she still continued to question the good news we brought her. But she was a good student. Our sharing of the gospel had not fallen on deaf ears. She took our lessons of love and our witness to the grace of God and tucked them away into the deep recesses of her excellent mind and memory. Nothing we had told her had been lost, only stowed away for a later day.

Nor had the campus changed.

We seemed to pick up our classes just where we had left them. But a new attitude had emerged. Instead of tighter restrictions, a new sense of freedom seemed to permeate the campus. Loren was asked to give night lectures to a group of businessmen who anticipated going to America on joint-venture business trips for their various companies.

"Do you have textbooks?" he asked the dean of the foreign language department.

When the answer was no, he was momentarily at a loss.

"What do you want me to tell them?" he asked.

"Lecture on anything you like," the dean replied.

"American life and culture. American home and family life. Religion."

Loren was both dumbfounded and elated. If ever there was an opportunity to witness, this was it. As a Christian teacher, he related the influence of Christianity on education. He was able to share with them that the first public education in America was done to teach children to read the Bible and to establish their lives on biblical principles. As we were Christian parents, he told about raising children in a Christian home and the overcoming power of a Christian marriage. Loren was permitted to talk, above all, about religion! He felt free to witness about the Lord and what He had done in our lives.

China was rife with propaganda about marriage in America. The students had been told that almost all marriages end in divorce. This is not shocking to them because of their government's attitude toward marriage. But our students had a problem equating this rumor about divorce with what they saw of us. They knew we had been married for over 40 years. They could see that we were still in love. And we were able to tell them that our four children also had Christian homes and Christian marriages. When young people came to us for advice concerning life questions about establishing homes and making good marriages, we gave them what we considered the secret of a successful marriage.

"It is easy to break one stick," we told them.

"It is harder to break two sticks bound together."

"But it is very difficult to break three sticks."

"When two of you are bound together in love, you will be strong. But when a third person is added, the Holy Spirit, it's almost impossible to break the marriage."

In addition to our regular classes, we were asked to give open lectures at night to all who were interested in life in America. We told them what we knew best. No need to talk about the corruption which is everywhere in the world. We told them that our lives were home- and church-centered. Sharing with them how we lived, we told of family altars, where we read the Bible to our children daily. We told them of opportunities we had of witnessing to our students at school. We shared with them our sense of responsibility for active participation in our church. Assuring them that life is not always easy in America, we could tell them that our faith made our lives stronger. They believed us because they had watched us and they had seen that it was the Lord Who held our lives and our marriage in His hands.

School and fellowship with our friends and students went smoothly. A very important friend in our lives was President Li.

He and Loren had become friends, accustomed to visiting when they met on the sidewalk outside our building. President Li loved to talk with Loren, practicing his English. And Loren loved to talk with him. If we had a good and supportive friend in China, it was President Li. Because of him, we were honored guests at lovely banquets.

The president was impressed by our youthfulness. He liked the way we dressed. He admired Loren's big belt with its large buckle, and he approved of my appearance. One of my favorite dresses was a wine-colored crepe. With my white hair, the color must have been startling to the Chinese whose elderly women cropped their dark hair and dressed primarily in drab, boxy pantsuits. But this style of dressing was changing for the younger women who were rapidly adopting Western fashions.

"Why don't you dress in colorful dresses like the American teacher?" the president asked his wife.

During one of the banquets that last spring, he encouraged us to eat the shellfish that we had always turned away from. Teaching Loren how to extract the flesh from the shell became his primary activity that night. That shell came to hold special importance for Loren, who kept it and brought it home. It is now in my kitchen window along with the figure of Dutch children.

From that night on, our friendship with President Li took on an almost intimate quality. He shared with us what he had said to his wife about us.

"They must love each other very much," he had observed. "They always walk holding hands."

We were still walking in joy, but our private life hit a snag. Loren had a problem that had begun in America at Christmastime. He had developed what he thought to be an ulcer. With medication, it seemed to improve. But the ulcer didn't heal because it wasn't an ulcer at all. It was the new tumor pressing against his stomach and back.

As his condition deteriorated in China, he began to suffer at night with severe itching on his back. Night after night, sitting on the edge of the bed, he would lean over the radiator as I gently scratched his back until he found relief or I fell asleep. He began to go to the school clinic, never telling them of his cancer. They doctored him with their ancient medicines, giving him herbs and ginseng root. But nothing helped. After many pain-filled days and sleepless nights, we asked that he be taken to the doctors at the Friendship Hospital for foreigners, hoping they would give him something for the itching.

There, though the technology seemed 50 years behind ours, the Chinese doctors, with their sensitive fingers, immediately discovered the tumor and diagnosed his problem for what it was. As one probed gently, he looked up at his associate and said, "I found a mass."

Loren and I looked at each other in dismay. The jig was up.

He was admitted to the hospital where, for several days, they administered their medicines to no effect. When they found that they could not help him, we knew we should return home. With great loving concern, although we had been back less than a semester, the university dismissed our classes and booked our passage back to America.

Our last day in Dalian seemed to be a repeat of the previous spring. Against the doctor's wishes, Loren insisted that he be allowed to return to our apartment so that he could see his students once more.

"I will not leave until I have told them good-bye!" he declared.

Back in our apartment, the students came to us in shock. With breaking hearts, we held them as we wept. We encouraged them not to leave the faith they had found, to cling together, support each other, and lend themselves to a better Teacher than we were, the Holy Spirit.

We prayed for them as they prayed for us. This time, we knew we would never see them again.

Once more, as we left the guesthouse, President Li and the party chairman were waiting for us in the lobby. Again they gave us parting gifts. And again they said those treasured words that meant so much.

But this time they did not invite us to return.

"Send us someone like yourselves," they said. "We have never had anyone love our students the way you do."

Although our classes had been canceled, a large gathering of our students had been called so that we could tell them good-bye. At first, as we stepped up to the platform, we couldn't speak for weeping. Loren's businessmen wept as hard as the rest of the students. When Loren felt he had control of his emotions, he began to speak. But his voice broke and he could not go on.

"You'll have to tell them, honey," he said, turning to me.

With my arm around him to support him, and with my own voice choking, I told them again our message of love. "We told you that love brought us to China. But never forget. It isn't our love, it's God's love. We came back so that you would know that love is real!"

There were many traumatic days to follow, but that day was perhaps the most painful day of our lives. We left China, but China would never leave us. We had experienced God's miraculous love at work there. And being used of God to bring the message of His love had been the crowning work of our lives.

We did not leave Dalian alone. Our friends from the Foreign Affairs Office went with us to Beijing where we were to catch a flight to Shanghai and then change to a plane for America. Whether it was necessary, or a part of their loving send-off for us, they gave us a three-day holiday in Beijing, providing sight-seeing salted with shopping for souvenirs to take home. We enjoyed a glorious meal at the famous Peking Duck Restaurant, a building several stories high which contains nothing but dining rooms in which to serve the world-famous dinners. Loren loved to hunt, and we had often eaten wild game at home. But we had never tasted anything like this!

Our departure from Beijing was especially painful. Accustomed to the emotions of our students, we were surprised at the travail our adult friends experienced. Never had we imagined that they loved us like they did. Xiuzhen had to be torn from our arms and held in restraint as we departed from her sight. Only one incident lightened the gloom of that day.

In the airport duty-free shop Loren made his last purchase in China. It was a kneeling Chinese soldier carved in stone, a replica of an ancient Xian man. Today it sits in an honored place in my home, a symbol of the promise that one day all China will kneel at the throne of God. Someday "every knee shall bow . . . and every tongue confess that Jesus Christ is Lord, to the glory of God the Father" (Phil. 2:10,11 NIV).

Our seats aboard the flight to Shanghai were crowded, and Loren, in extreme discomfort, had difficulty adjusting to the situation. We knew we were in for a long flight. I was distraught to think of his suffering all that way.

Shortly before boarding, our friends had handed me a letter to give to the attendants on our flight. Not being able to read Chinese, we had no idea what it said. When we boarded in Beijing, I handed the letter to the stewardess who was busy and tucked it in her pocket. Later she came to us in distress. The letter, it seemed, stated that Loren was a man highly respected by the national Bureau of Foreign Affairs, and being gravely ill, he should receive every possible consideration. Apologizing, she informed us that there were no extra seats available on our flight. But in Shanghai, things would be different. And they were.

Upon boarding the huge 747 for Los Angeles, we were led to the last row in our section where there were six empty seats. We were to have all six. Insisting that Loren lie down, the lovely attendants brought him pillows and blankets, plying him with fruit juices and liquids, and constantly checking on his condition. No better care could have been given him on any flight. Still in a great deal of discomfort, he was able to sleep much of the way across the Pacific.

My discomfort was of a different kind. My heart was grieving over my husband's pain. But my soul was in torment because we seemed to have misunderstood the Lord's leading in coming back to China.

"Why," I cried out to Him, "did you let us come back when you knew Loren was so sick and we could not stay?"

With loving-kindness, the Spirit whispered softly to me: "You did what I sent you to do."

The response meant nothing to me then, but my soul became quiet. It was enough. It was months later, after Loren was gone, that I understood the full meaning of those words.

22

I Touch the Scales

"I have planted, Apollos watered; but God gave the increase" (1 Cor. 3:6 KJV).

We were once again at home on the shores of the lake. Our mission to China was finished. We knew that we would never go back again.

Loren, with massive doses of chemotherapy and painkillers, was feeling better. The doctor assured us that he could bring the lymphoma under control.

Our spirits were finally at rest. But our hearts were still in China.

There were those we saw born into the kingdom who needed to be nurtured. There were those who, like King Agrippa, were "almost persuaded." And there were those who were just beginning to inquire into the love and joy, the why that had brought us to China.

But we had peace in our spirits and could say with Paul, "I have planted, Apollos watered; but God gave the increase."

Soon letters began to arrive from those we had left behind on the other side of the world.

We were missed.

How was Dad?

Had the doctors done anything for him?
When were we coming back?

Carrie wrote of her joy at our return and her pain at our leaving again.

"I was very excited when you came back. Because of last May's action, the future of our nation is not promising. We were worried about the future of our country as well as our own. I thought maybe there were no foreign teachers who would come back.

"Then you came back, saying, 'Here we are!' With this sentence it seemed sunshine came back, hope came back, happiness came back.

"One day, after class, I asked Mrs. Notley how to escape from loneliness. You told me to love others.

"You went back with your smile. Your voice left here.

"In the morning before becoming awake completely, I ask myself, 'What's the class today? Is there Notley?'

"No, I tell myself. On the campus there will not be these days again. Here, there is not their laughter of happiness, not lectures again.

"They are far away."

After returning home, we were busy with Loren's treatments. But we were determined not to lose touch with those we had left behind in China. As letters flew back and forth, the love songs and heart's cries of our students filled the mails.

Donna repeated her song of love.

"What a pity we couldn't have your class anymore.

"What a pity that we couldn't celebrate your 43 years of marriage.

"Whenever I mention your happy marriage to others, almost everybody admires you. How happy you are. When I was at home on June 16, I said to my parents that day was our foreign teachers' commemoration day of 43 years of marriage. I can only say my best wish for you at home.

"Could you hear me? Wish you happiness forever!

"How I miss you!

"Please come back to China!

"I love you!"

Virginia wrote, and together with Donna, it was a duet of love.

"Dear Notleys:

"Whenever I greet the sunrise and sunset with a happy praise song, whenever I hold my precious gift in my hands and read it, you appear just before me. Never will I forget the tears we shed at the farewell party, nor the nights in your apartment which were the most fruitful and joyous time to me during that spring.

"You were with us for only a short time, but how much this short period meant to me. I was so much encouraged by your deep faith and love and so much encouraged by your patient and plain explanation of the deep truth that I found myself grow up rapidly in our beloved Father.

"Thank you for the love you brought to me! For to us you are the window through which we see the outside world.

"We respect Mr. Notley as a humorous and excellent teacher. We admire Mrs. Notley as an example we'd like to follow: graceful, adroit, strong in dealing with all sorts of problems, rich in experiencing all kinds of tastes. And we especially consider your marriage as happy and harmonious, the very kind of marriage we long to possess in the future.

"You are not only our teachers of our textbooks, more important, you are our spiritual teachers. How much we wanted to have those nights happen again.

"My dear teachers, I understood that whether you will come back or not depends on the Almighty Power. He will arrange for us. With this faith, I keep the love and hope in my heart. For I know I'm deeply loved, not only by the people around us but also by you who are far away on the other side of the Pacific Ocean. No matter what happens, you are in my sincere love and prayers.

"Thank you for bringing love to my world!"

In the wealth of mail we received was a parcel from Barbara and her friend Jonathan. It was a pair of beautiful Chinese scrolls. There were no pictures this time, only Chinese characters spelling out a message we could not read. They were a gift for our wedding anniversary. With them came a letter of interpretation.

The left scroll said: "Being LianLee on the Earth: A kind of tree whose roots join together—a couple deeply in love."

The right scroll said, "Being Flying Birds in the Heaven: Two birds flying high in the sky."

◆

As the summer progressed, so did Loren's cancer. Treatments and surgery failed to halt its progress. In early September, he was hospitalized for the last time.

Determined that no spirit of death invade his room, I prayed that the Lord would take up residence there. Faithful to the last, He was ever-present at Loren's side. Friends who came to minister to him went away filled with awe at the strong sense of the presence of the Lord in that room.

At times when we were alone, I would sit on the side of his bed, gazing into his clear blue eyes.

I told him how much I loved him.

I told him how much our life together had meant to me.

I kissed his dear face.

With his own unwavering gaze, he seemed to drink in my face as if to hold it in his memory for eternity. At other times he gazed past me at something I could not see.

Sometimes in the deep hours of the night, when the pain wracked his body, I would crawl into bed with him and hold him like a little child, singing to him about Jesus. At the name of Jesus, he would become still and peaceful. Our Lord was there.

"Honey," I told him at the last, "I envy you. You get to see Jesus first!"

Loren had loved music. His life had been a song of praise. And now we were determined that his room should resound with the hymns he loved so much. Our daughters, Kathy and Laura, brought in a cassette player and tapes, and hour after hour the soft music swirled about his bed, bringing peace and comfort to his tortured body.

Once, when the strains of "Victory in Jesus" were filling the room, I noticed that his lips were moving although he was too weak to speak. Intent on knowing what he was trying to say, I put my ear near his mouth.

He was singing "Victory in Jesus."

"I have to get well!" he had declared all summer. "I have to go back to China!"

Like Paul, he was determined that "none of these things move me, neither count I my life dear unto myself, so that I might finish my course with joy, and the ministry which I have received from the Lord Jesus, to testify the gospel of the grace of God."

But one day all that changed. He realized that *his* course was finished.

"How are you doing, buddy?" the doctor asked him.

"I just want to go home," he whispered. His heavenly home.

In late September, the Lord took him home.

Ours had been a long marriage with its problems and its victories. But through all the happy years and through all the turbulent times, we had grown stronger and closer together. We had finished our life together on the greatest honeymoon anyone could ever imagine.

With the Lord as our guide, we had gone to China!

23

For China and for Thee

"Father, protect them by the power of your name" (John 17:11 NIV).

In China, we felt we had broken virgin soil and planted the word of God. We prayed that we had laid a solid foundation upon which others could build. It was now up to the Lord of the harvest to send laborers into His harvest.

After Loren had gone, letters of comfort began to arrive from China. Those who knew him and loved him began to write about the influence he had on their lives. The messages were sometimes overpowering. Perhaps the greatest joy was learning that they were growing in the word and in the Lord, and that they were moving on with their lives.

Paul, that brilliant young writer whom the Lord had so gloriously anointed as he learned to pray the Lord's Prayer, wrote soon after Loren's death, not knowing he had gone.

"I want to see you again and pray with you for Mr. Notley."

"On Christmas Eve I will pray God to bless you and your family! I miss you. I cannot forget the time we spent together."

The power of prayer had made an impact on his young life.

We knew that there were those the Lord would anoint for use in His service. It was not always those we thought He was touching at first. Although many of our students came to the Lord, His special calling sometimes surprised us. On the eve of the Tiananmen Square massacre, I would never have dreamed He had His hand upon Shirley.

Shirley, that precious girl who had despaired of her life once, had turned her eyes upon the Lord instead of the world around her.

"How much I miss you and need you during this period of study when I find no explainers and teachers around me."

"I need you, not only in courses but in spiritual work as well.

"It was really the happiest time when we were together, sharing love and happiness. And your encouragement of 'Make something of your life' impressed me indeed. I found a large potential inside me, ready to make something for China and the world. I can lay my hand on the Bible, from which I have undergone an experience of Holy Spirit. And all these, I believe, are offered by God through you."

Later she was to write from Jutland, Denmark.

"I am now studying in a mini Bible school. It was very difficult to come out of China. But the Lord blessed and opened the door. The last 17 months I have been living by faith, trusting Him for everything day by day.

"The Lord is so faithful. I have tasted His goodness. He is so good.

"It was a key time when we were together in China. Do you know how important a role you have played in the life of a young girl?"

Virginia's letters read like something out of the epistles of Paul.

"'How beautiful are the feet of those who bring the good news' is the verse I loved very much after the departure of you. Yes, how beautiful are your feet which brought us the good news of love and peace. You planted the seeds in our hearts and carefully watered the soil.

"We must build faith in the hearts of those who doubt, we must rekindle faith in ourselves when it grows dim, and find some kind of divine courage within us to keep on until on earth we have peace and goodwill among men.

"No ray of sunlight is ever lost, but the green which it wakes needs time to sprout and it is not always granted to the sower to see the harvest.

"All work that is worth anything is done in faith."

There were words of love and comfort for Loren's passing.

"We all love Mr. Notley dearly," she wrote, "and both of you are brought to our minds quite often. Even knowing about his passing away, we still love to talk about him. I hold that his life in China has been so successful that he attracted lots of love and admiration from the students, and I also believe his whole life has been a fulfilling one. Otherwise we wouldn't see half so much love for him.

"My heart ached to think of the solitary struggle that is going on with you. You are in the "deep thought" of all of us here who believe.

"Blessed are those who mourn.

"I will be the husband to the widow.

"Rejoice in hope, patient in tribulation."

These words came from one who might rightfully expect sorrow and tribulation in her own life in the aftermath of her country's massacre that took so many young lives. It humbled me. When I read these words again years later, I rejoiced to know that my grief must have been lessened by the prayers and petitions of those left behind in China.

Virginia went through her own time of testing. Months later she wrote:

"Five months after you departed was my darkest period in life. Feeling like an orphan sheep, I even questioned what the point it was to live in a world of wolves. I wondered, struggled, cried out. No direct answer came to me, but deep down in my heart I knew I could not give up life. There was a calling from above to encourage me to hold on.

"'A bruised reed he will not break, and a smoldering wick he will not snuff out' is a dear Scripture to me, for it perfectly describes my life at that point.

"No cloud can forever cover the sunshine.

"I found there was a severe struggle in my heart between spirit and flesh. I discovered I was such a wretch, such as failure, I questioned why with a desire to be good and loving, I actually did what I hated to do.

"One day when I was reading a book by Watch-man Nee, the words struck my heart: 'How can you expect a builder to build you a house without giving him building materials? How can you expect a tailor to make you a coat without giving him cloth? In the same way, how can you expect "Father" to build in you the character of His Son without presenting yourself to Him?' [paraphrased]

"Finally I understood why I failed Him. I did not give up control of my life to Him. I did not put Him first in my life, learning to die to my old nature daily.

"Father has been so faithful to lead me from one fresh victory to another, though I constantly make mistakes.

"I have wanted to write to you but I feared it would cause you sorrow. Suddenly I remembered one evening when you, Mr. Notley, Shirley, and I were talking.

"You said, 'I am not walking in fear although I know there are restrictions. For perfect love casts out all fear.'

"I appreciate your loving heart for China. Your work for Him was not in vain. It produced fruit, though it took great patience to wait and see it.

"He will be with me and I will follow and serve Him at whatever cost."

The messages from Eugene were not so glorious. Separated from the small body of believers which had held each other up at the university, he seemed to be cast adrift upon the rivers of China. Soon after our final return we had attempted to help him go to a Bible school in the Philippines. But it was useless. He would not be permitted to leave the country. With letters and love, we attempted to encourage him. He wrote:

"Dear Mom and Dad:
"I heard that you brought me a beautiful Bible. Thanks for your profound care. I like the Book of Job. From this book I get a lot to think about. Job suffered for no reason. Through this, God showed His glory. We don't understand for we are nothing. We won't get the truth unless by God. Pray for me and strengthen me."

In my heart, I knew God had His hand on Eugene. And I continued to believe that "God's gifts and his call are irrevocable." There is a work for Eugene to do. God called him. He will use him yet in spreading the gospel across China.

The final victory over which I rejoiced was with Barbara. We had sent her letters, both written and oral, and music tapes, through which the Holy Spirit worked as He had not been able to work through us.

Barbara was alone; and though she didn't realize it at the time, the Holy Spirit, the Lord of the harvest, was with her, reaping the seed we had sown. She wrote:

"Dear Mom:
"I'm not the Barbara you knew as before. It happened to me this Sunday.

"I was listening to the music tapes at the moment when I heard these words: ''Tis so sweet to trust in Jesus, Just to take Him at His word . . .'

"I was deeply moved. I cried because I felt a crushing guilt not believing in Him. I realized that I had been lost for such a long time and I was aware of my weakness and His power. I cried so hard that I almost couldn't stand this. Oh, Mom, I hadn't ever had that feeling before. So badly I longed for Him to save me! For the first time I confessed and thanked Him for letting me have the opportunity of change. I prayed that night, felt more peaceful and inner strength. So I'd like you to share my happiness and pleasure.

"It is you and dear Dad who made all this possible. Maybe he was an ordinary man in the world, but he played an extraordinary role in my life.

"I love you, Mom. I now know much more about how to love and be loved. Thank the Lord for letting me have such a super Mom.

"I love you. Barbara"

What a joy! How it made my heart sing to know that our sweet Barbara had finally met the Lord and committed her heart to Him! It was what we had been praying for all the time, and it made the short time we spent in China all worthwhile.

In my spirit He said to me: "See, you didn't need to be there. I was there. All I asked of you was to plant the seed. It was up to Me to reap the harvest."

Barbara eventually came to America, went to Bible school, and married. How God loves her! He sent His Word to her. He has great plans in store for one He loves so much.

We touched many students' lives, and it is not possible to know how many were changed. It is not necessary that we know. We claimed one. We got many.

It was the testimony of one we left behind that put the final stamp on what we did.

"When you left after Tiananmen Square, we thought you were just soft Americans. But when you came back, and Dad was so sick, but you came back anyway to tell us God's love was real, then we knew that what you said was true."

On the plane going home He had said to me: "You did what I sent you to do."

Now I understood.

Only in eternity, as we stand before the throne and the books are opened, will we know which of our precious students came into the kingdom with us.

We had seen dark days, but we felt that the darkness would eventually end. Sensing that God was doing something great in China, we claimed the harvest for Him. The revolution was not simply political, but it is, even now, a great spiritual battle for the soul of China.

China had opened her doors. The revival that had been going on for many years among the peasants is pouring out over the campuses of the colleges and universities. Here is being implanted into the hearts of the "cream" of China, her youth, a hunger which we pray will never go away.

And the revival, which we sensed so strongly was coming, will eventually awaken that old sleeping dragon called China, and sweep like wildfire across her rice fields and her cities; and our Lord will claim China for His own.